UNDERSTANDING BE

RELATED MACMILLAN TITLES

For GNVQ/Applied Intermediate Business:

Intermediate GNVQ Business, Helen Turner and Francis Nicholson
Intermediate GNVQ Business: City & Guilds Option Units,
   S. K. Davies

For GNVQ/Applied Advanced Business:

Advanced GNVQ Business, Arlene Mary Jones and Geraint Rees
Advanced GNVQ Financial Services Today, Daphne Turner, Peter
   Turner and Philip Voysey
Advanced GNVQ Financial Planning and Monitoring, David Sutton,
   Daphne Turner and Peter Turner

ADVANCED GNVQ
Understanding
Behaviour at Work

Judith Bourne

MACMILLAN

First published 1997 by
MACMILLAN PRESS LTD
Houndmills, Basingstoke, Hampshire RG21 6XS
and London
Companies and representatives
throughout the world

ISBN 0–333–67988–1

A catalogue record for this book is available
from the British Library.

This book is printed on paper suitable for recycling and made from fully managed and sustained forest sources.

10   9   8   7   6   5   4   3   2   1
06   05   04   03   02   01   00   99   98   97

Copy-edited and typeset by Povey–Edmondson
Okehampton and Rochdale, England

Printed in Hong Kong

Contents

List of Cases

Cases 10, 11, 12 and 16 were written with the cooperation and approval of the companies concerned. Cases 5 and 14 are reproduced with the permission of *Personnel Today*. Case 8 is reproduced with the permission of the Institute of Administrative Management. Case 13 is reproduced with the permission of the John Lewis Partnership.

Preface

The primary aim of this book is to meet the requirements of the Applied Advanced Business unit *Behaviour at Work* (BTEC) but it also covers areas of *Working in Teams* and *Management* (RSA) and *Methods and Channels of Business Communication* (City and Guilds). It also provides an introduction for anyone interested in obtaining a practical understanding of working with or managing people at work.

The Introduction sets the scene for the book but thereafter the three parts may be studied independently and in any order. Each part includes a portfolio assignment, aimed at the requirements of the evidence indicators. The nature of the assignments (and the point at which each should be commenced) may influence the order in which the three parts are studied at school or college.

A wide range of activities are included to provide an opportunity to:

- Reflect on the topics.
- Collect documentary evidence for portfolios.
- Apply personal experiences and the case material.

The cases are based on real as well as fictional organisations and situations. The real-life studies form a vital part of the book by setting the study of behaviour at work within the context of today's world of business and industry.

Links with Other Units

	BTEC *Behaviour at Work*	RSA *Working in Teams*	RSA *Management*	C&G *Methods and Channels of Business Communication*
	Unit 11	Unit 12	Unit 22	Unit 11

INTRODUCTION

1	Introduction	Background knowledge and preparation – all units

PART A: INVESTIGATING MANAGEMENT STYLES 11.1

2	Development of Management	Supporting and background knowledge – all units			
3	Management Styles	11.1.1	12.1.5	22.1.5/6	
4	Role and Responsibilities of the Manager	11.1.2	12.1.5	22.1.1	
5	Managers and Communication	11.1.3	12.1.2/4	22.1.3/4	11.1/11.2

PART B: INVESTIGATING THE EFFECTS OF MOTIVATION ON PERFORMANCE 11.2

6	Attitudes to Work	11.2.1	Background	Background	
7	Factors Affecting Motivation	11.2.2	12.1.4	22.1.2	
8	Motivators at Work	11.2.3	12.1.4	22.1.2	

PART C: EXAMINING THE BEHAVIOUR OF GROUPS IN THE WORKPLACE 11.3 12.2/3*

9	The Nature of Groups	11.3.1	12.1.6	22.1.6	
10	Roles in Groups	11.3.2	12.1.6		
11	Group Behaviour	11.3.3	12.1.6		
12	Making Groups Work	11.3.4	12.1.6		

Notes:
11.1.2 indicates Unit 11, Element 1, Performance Criteria 1.
*the portfolio assignment for Part C (Method A, Tasks 1 and 2) could also form the basis for the business activity prescribed for Elements 2 and 3 of *Working in Teams*.

About the Author

Judith Bourne worked as an administrator in both the public services and private industry before becoming a further education lecturer in business and management. She now works as a freelance writer, lecturer and administrator.

Acknowledgements

The author would like to thank the following for their generous help and assistance: Paul Greenall and CARNAUDMETALBOX; John Haines of Isle College, Wisbech; John Jackman; Mary Jones of Jones PR; John Loasby and Campbell Grocery Products Ltd; Stephen Rutt, John Winckler and Macmillan Press; Jonathan Street and Lands' End Direct Merchants Ltd; Roger Ward and Tulip International A/S; and Keith Bourne for his advice, encouragement and support.

The author is also grateful to the following for permission to reproduce material from their publications: The Institute of Administrative Management, The John Lewis Partnership and *Personnel Today*.

INTRODUCTION
BEHAVIOUR AT WORK

1 INTRODUCTION

1.1 THE OBJECTIVES

The main aim of this book is to meet the performance criteria of the GNVQ advanced optional unit, *Behaviour at Work*.

To provide you with the necessary background knowledge, the text outlines the major theories about how people behave in their working lives. It uses case material to illustrate the theory and link it to the presentday workplace. The case material also enables you to view aspects of behaviour and the organisation's use of behavioural approaches within a realistic context. Most of this material is taken from real organisations who have kindly provided detailed information and agreed its use.

The book also encourages you to draw on your own experience: the study of behaviour becomes an immensely practical subject when it is related to one's own behaviour and experience. The activities give you, the student, the opportunity to investigate and research your behaviour and that of others in different situations, and, if you are studying this book as part of a GNVQ programme, to build up evidence that you have fulfilled the performance criteria set down for the unit. Each of the three parts contains a portfolio assignment that meets the GNVQ evidence indicators for that element.

When learning about business, try to relate the different aspects of business and the business world to each other. Within the GNVQ business programme it is useful to be able to see where the units you are studying link up or overlap each other. Links with other units are therefore identified in the text to help you make connections with your learning in other parts of the programme. Also highlighted are activities that could provide opportunities for you to claim evidence of the use of core skills. Unless stated otherwise, references are to units and core skills for Advanced GNVQ in Business.

3

1.2   ABOUT THE BOOK

It is important, as a starting point, to understand what we are studying in this book. For example it is *not* intended to provide a set of rules about *how* to behave at work. Rather the book examines the *why* of behaviour. For example, why do individuals usually respond better to praise than to criticism? If we understand why people behave in a certain way we have a greater chance of working with them in harmony, without friction. Understanding behaviour does not always solve the problems resulting from it but it may help us to deal with those problems – or at least, in some circumstances, to accept that we have to live with them.

1.3   BEHAVIOUR

At this stage you may be asking what exactly is meant by 'behaviour'. How you behave is essentially how you conduct yourself, how you act, but equally important to behaviour are the circumstances in which you and the other people involved find yourselves. Behaviour is very complex and follows few rules.

Predicting

Sometimes we feel we can tell in advance exactly how a person will act in certain circumstances. More often than not, however, we are surprised because that person does not act in the way we expected. Parents are constantly surprised by their offspring, spouses by their partners, and so on. If we cannot even correctly predict the behaviour of our 'nearest and dearest', whom we claim to know well, what chance have we of predicting the behaviour of others?

ACTIVITY 1.1   Think of a situation in which someone you know very well did not act in the way you expected, then make notes as follows:

1.   Outline the situation.
2.   Describe what the person did.
3.   Describe what you expected her/him to do and why you expected her/him to behave in that way.
4.   Do you know of any reason why that person acted in the way she/he did at that particular time?

Expectations

Behaviour is further complicated because we have expectations of how people *should* behave.

For example a young man sees a small boy playing by the river. There is no other person in sight. The small boy slips and falls into the river. What would you expect the young man to do? Try to pull the child out? Run for help? But what if the young man simply turned and walked away. How would you feel about that?

Expectations of certain types of behaviour may be governed by ideas of morality (it's wrong to cheat), the conventions of a particular society (queuing to be served in a shop), the rules of an organisation (some restaurants will not admit men who are not wearing a jacket and tie), or in some cases the law (motor cyclists must wear crash helmets).

ACTIVITY 1.2   Give six more examples of expected behaviour, describing the circumstances and the reasons for the expected behaviour.

Causes

Why do we behave the way we do? Mentioned above are some situations where there is an expected form of behaviour. But what else affects the way you as an individual behave? What makes you into a person different from all others?

- *Inheritance.* We all inherit certain characteristics and physical attributes from our parents. We are influenced by the genes passed on to us. You may have eyes like your father, a quick temper like your mother, a nose that your grandmother says is just like your Uncle Fred's! This is often referred to as the influence of *nature* on the way we are.
- *Upbringing.* Sociologists refer to this as *nurture* and look to the environment and influences of our early years. This includes our home and family background, for example, whether our home was in a rural area or a city, the financial situation of our family and the culture of the community in which we lived, its values, customs and accepted forms of behaviour.
- *Direct influences.* These are the influences closest to us. For example the beliefs of our parents, our relationship with our siblings, friends, teachers perhaps, and spouse or partner.
- *Indirect influences.* These stem from the society and world in which we live and may arise from, for example, 'fashionable'

ideas of the time, popular beliefs, attitudes displayed in the press, things we see on television or read in books and magazines. We may be influenced by public figures – be it a pop star or a prime minister.

- *Personal experiences*. Each of us is affected by our experiences. These will change or affect our future behaviour in some way – sometimes only slightly (perhaps by reinforcing what we believe) but sometimes in a dramatic way. For example people who have suffered a serious illness or have been involved in an accident are often heard to say that it changed their whole attitude to life – they have a different perspective of what is important to them and what does not really matter.

- *Other circumstances*. Most of us are affected by combinations of events, often completely outside our control, that affect even the smallest aspect of our everyday life and set up a flow of circumstances that influence how we react. For example a shop assistant misses the bus and consequently is late for work. This gets her into trouble with her supervisor. Her annoyance at missing the bus is now compounded by a 'telling off' and may well spill over into her dealings with customers that morning – until perhaps another event changes her mood or pattern of behaviour. Worries at home may make it difficult for us to concentrate on our studies and for a time lower grades are achieved. A new relationship may fill our thoughts and we daydream when we should be giving our attention to our work.

ACTIVITY 1.3 Build up a brief profile of yourself by identifying certain aspects of your personality and behaviour that arise out of each of the categories listed below:

- Inheritance
- Upbringing
- Direct influences
- Indirect influences
- Personal experiences.

Identify an event in the past twenty-four hours that caused you to behave in a particular way or invoked a particular mood.

ACTIVITY 1.4 Group Discussion: To what extent is behaviour influenced by the media (television, the press and so on)?

Core skill:
communication

Effects

What is the effect of behaviour in a work context? Does it matter what one individual says or does? The following examples demonstrate, in simple terms, the effects of one person's behaviour on others and the possible outcomes of that behaviour.

	Behaviour	Possible effects
Example 1:	A shop assistant is rude to a customer, and unhelpful.	The customer is offended and does not buy. She or he associates that shop with the rude assistant and does not go there again. If the pattern is repeated with other customers, business may decline.
Example 2:	A shop assistant is very helpful and pleasant.	The customer is more inclined to buy. She or he will associate shop with the helpful assistant and is encouraged to return. If this pattern is repeated with all customers, business is likely to improve.
Example 3:	A manager is always critical of a particular worker, rarely giving praise or encouragement and says the worker is useless.	The employee becomes nervous and makes more mistakes. His or her performance declines further.
Example 4:	A manager hands out praise when work is good. When performance is less good, the manager offers help and encouragement in order to bring about an improvement.	The employee responds to the praise and tries harder to succeed and improve, thus receiving more praise. The employee continues to develop her or his skills.

Examples 3 and 4 illustrate how patterns of behaviour can develop, creating a circle or spiral. In Example 3 both parties may find it difficult to break out of the spiral and both the relationship between the two and the employee's performance will continue to decline. Ultimately the employee will probably leave or be dismissed – both organisation and employee lose in this situation. In Example 4, however, support and help when needed and praise for achievement will encourage the worker to develop – to the advantage of both the organisation and the employee.

1.4   WORK

The second word in the book title to which we need to give some thought is work. The word 'work' is very much part of our everyday language but we use it in a variety of contexts. For example:

- She *works* in a bank.
- The television set is broken; it won't *work*.
- Digging the garden is hard *work*.
- He does a lot of *work* for the church.
- People *work* for a living.
- A person is '*work* shy'.

It is therefore important that we understand what 'work' means in the context of behaviour at work. In fact we need to ask two questions:

- What is work?
- Why do we work?

What is work?

ACTIVITY 1.5   Look at the following list and write down the letters preceding the examples you would describe as 'work':

(A)   Taking notes in class.
(B)   Filling up shelves in a supermarket.
(C)   Washing up after a meal at home.
(D)   Serving at the local cafe.
(E)   Helping to organise a car boot sale to raise funds for the youth club.
(F)   Taking part in football practice ready for the game on Saturday.

Write down your reasons for choosing or not choosing each example.

Which did you select? How did you make your choice?

It's difficult, isn't it? Is it work only if you are paid? In that case the answer to (F) would depend on whether you were a professional footballer or played for a school or college. Is it work when the task requires effort? Is it work when you do something you don't really enjoy or have to do?

Consider the situation described in the following case.

CASE 1 LEE   Lee is a trainee gardener in the local Parks Department and has always wanted to be a gardener. Unfortunately he and his parents live in a flat so have no garden, but most Sundays he looks after the garden of an old lady who lives nearby. She is no longer able to tend it herself and cannot afford to pay anyone to do it for her. Lee would love a garden of his own where no one tells him what to put in it or where. He and the old lady have therefore come to a very satisfactory arrangement – she gets her garden looked after and Lee gets to do what he wants. The garden has been neglected for a long time, and clearing it of weeds, rubbish, stones and so on is what Lee describes as a 'hard slog'.

The question is: when is Lee working?

- Is he working only when he is paid to do so?
- Is he working when he considers it to be a 'hard slog', involving unpleasant effort?
- Is he working when he starts planning the layout of the garden, that is, what he sees as the enjoyable part?

This provides an interesting aspect of our concept of work for it appears that we carry out different types of work:

- Work for which we are paid (employment).
- Work we undertake on a purely voluntary basis, perhaps for a particular organisation, for which we are not paid (voluntary or charitable work).
- Work we have to do, whether we like it or not, and for which we are not paid (for example housework, washing the car, homework).
- Work for which we are not paid but undertake simply because we enjoy it (for example helping to restore old steam engines for a railway preservation society).

Consequently we all undertake a variety of activities that we call work: sometimes we work in return for payment; some work we undertake as a duty because we feel we must do it or it is a necessary part of the life we lead; and there is work we choose to do for the good of others or simply because we enjoy it.

It is part of most of the cultures within our society that we work or in some other way fulfil an accepted work role (for example one partner looks after the home and children while the other works to provide income). We no longer believe that it is right for us to own slaves to do our work for us. In general our society expects people to be involved in some type of work or activity, paid or unpaid. Value is given to being a 'useful member of society'. Even after retirement most people express the need to feel useful and keep busy, even if at a more leisurely pace.

When we meet people for the first time we often ask, 'What do you do?', meaning the type of paid work they are involved in. We would probably be surprised if someone replied that he or she did not *choose* to do anything. The most common problem for those who are unemployed is a feeling of failure, loss of purpose and loss of awareness of who they are or their place in society. Many unemployed people find that the problems of 'not working' (as opposed to 'not earning') are lessened if they are involved in other activities. Even the very rich, who have no financial necessity to work, usually feel the need to be involved in some sort of activity to make them feel useful, whether it be managing their estates or participating in charity work.

However our society is constantly changing – the role of women, advances in technology, expectation of a longer life, changes in education. It is possible that recession and high unemployment levels will change society's expectations in relation to work too.

ACTIVITY 1.6   Increased unemployment levels mean that a larger proportion of the population will not be in paid employment for some or all of the time. Discuss in groups:

Core skill: communication

1.   How this affects our work culture (that is, the idea that most people will work).
2.   How this affects our 'identification' of people by the work they do.

Link: production and employment in the economy

Write your group's ideas on a flipchart or a large sheet of paper. At the end of 15 minutes, pin up each group's sheet and compare the results.

In the context of our study of behaviour at work we are in general considering work in relation to paid employment rather than any of the other aspects of work referred to above. Nevertheless it is important to be aware that paid work is not the only type that people do or consider a necessary part of their lives.

ACTIVITY 1.7

Link: production and employment in the economy

Working individually, write down your experiences of employment. This could be full-time, part-time or casual work. Describe briefly what your duties were, to whom you were responsible and how you were paid. If you have no experience of employment, describe either the employment of someone you know or the job you would like to do. Present your findings to the other members of your class.

ACTIVITY 1.8

Working in pairs, consult *one* of the following, so that within the class a range of different sources is covered:

- A local newspaper
- A local job centre
- A local employment agency

From your chosen source, obtain brief details of ten different jobs being advertised. Present your findings to the other members of your class and discuss the findings of the class as a whole. For example similarities or differences in:

Link: business organisations and employment (intermediate)

- The types of work advertised
- Experience required
- Pay levels
- Qualifications needed

Why Do We Work?

Our second question was why do we work? Looking at this in the context of work as paid employment, the usual reply is: for money. But is that strictly true? In reality our reasons for working are much more complex.

Even the answer 'for money' covers a variety of motives, since few of us are misers who want to amass money entirely for its own sake. (Where's the fun in simply sitting counting it!) Each of us will use the money we earn in different ways.

Some of the other reasons for working have already been touched upon: it is part of our society's culture, it gives us identity and purpose, it confers status, it affects both our physical and mental well-being. Let us now look in more detail at some of these points.

Money

If we assume that money is our primary reason for working, what is the importance of money to us?

- It enables us to buy essentials, that is, to feed and clothe ourselves and obtain somewhere to live.
- It gives us the opportunity to follow our interests, for example to go out with our friends, to change our clothes according to fashion, to follow a chosen sport or hobby.
- It may allow us to follow a particular life style. If we want a better or more costly standard of living, we may be able to save up for something in particular or look to see whether we can earn more money in another job.

CASE 2 Jasbindar   Jasbindar works in an office, and still lives with her parents. She has worked out that she will spend the money she earns in the following way.

Category 1:
- Board paid to mother.
- Lunch on days at work.
- Bus fares to and from work.
- Clothes, shoes and so on for work.
- Personal items: toiletries, shoe repairs and so on.

Category 2:
- Entertainment: social activities with friends, cinema visits, tapes and discs.
- Non-work clothes.
- Saving for a holiday.
- Christmas and birthday presents for family and friends.

Category 3:
- Saving to buy a car.

In the above case, the items in Category 1 are the essentials that Jasbindar knows she has to cover. Category 2 covers her social activities and interests, and other things she wants to do or have but are not essential. Category 3 indicates that Jasbindar wants to improve her life style in that she sees a car as giving her greater independence and the freedom to go where she wishes. It may be that later she will want to move into a place of her own or to share with friends, so she will put this into Category 3 when she feels she is reaching the necessary income to fulfil this objective.

ACTIVITY 1.9   Make a list of how you spend the money available to you. Then sort your list into those items you consider essential or necessary, those that are non-essential or leisure interests, and those you see as allowing you to follow a particular life style, either now or in the future.

Through our income we therefore aim to satisfy our essential needs, but we may also wish to satisfy other interests and aspirations.

Society

Adult humans have always needed to look after themselves and their familities, providing food, shelter and protection. In our society it is generally expected that when possible we will try to support ourselves and our dependents, and the proportion of adults that do not expect to be employed at some point in their lives has grown increasingly smaller. Many aspects of our education system are designed with future employment in mind. Most people do not like to be unemployed since this not only results in reduced income but also in loss of value within our society. Many unemployed people feel guilty and demoralised, even though they may be unemployed through no fault of their own.

Work is now seen as a major concern and goal in life in most industrialised areas of the world. Being unable to work, for whatever reasons, usually brings loss of identity and status. Only when an accepted retirement age is reached does society remove the obligation on the individual to work and take away the supposed stigma that many associate with not having a job.

ACTIVITY 1.10

Link: self-development for career planning; people in business organisations (intermediate)

1. Describe the type of work or job you would like to do.
2. What do you think will be the advantages to you of this type of work? For example career advancement, money to buy certain things or live in a particular way, important position, satisfying nature of the work.
3. Discuss and compare your views with others in a group or the class. Do you share similar objectives or do you all have different ambitions?

Needs

What do we mean by 'needs'? Needs are those things that are essential or important to us as individuals.

We can start by thinking of a baby's needs: to be fed regularly, to be kept warm and dry, to be safe and secure, and to be loved and cared for. As the baby begins to grow, she or he starts to learn how to communicate with and relate to others, to seek attention and approval for what she or he does. The baby begins to explore and investigate, demonstrating curiosity and a desire to find things out (what soil tastes like, what's behind that cupboard door). Adult human needs are a development of the baby's needs. We need food and clothing, and somewhere to live and call home. We are all familiar with the anxiety or fear we experience when we find ourselves in a strange place or surrounded by strangers – we like to feel safe and secure. We want friends – people who think like us and share our interests and activities – and to be loved. Most of us acknowledge that we also want others to like us, to think well of us, to show appreciation of our efforts.

Most people wish to achieve in something. For some, the challenge lies in climbing mountains or winning a place in the first team. Some will set goals to achieve the GNVQ Advanced or get a job, or both. It is obvious that many people never stop wanting to achieve something new, such as the 90-year-old who studies an A level or the 65-year-old who wants to try parachuting or sail round the world. We all set ourselves goals and age is no deterrent to wanting to extend what we do, what we know or what we are.

ACTIVITY 1.11   List five objectives that you wish to achieve within the next five years.

1.5   SUMMARY

- *Behaviour:* the way we act or conduct ourselves, influenced by our physical and genetic makeup, the environment we grew up in and live in, the people we know well, people we don't know and events outside our immediate lives, our personal experiences and the small everyday circumstances and incidents that happen to us.
- *Work*: paid employment that enables us to take a particular role in society and earn the money to satisfy some of our needs.
- *Personal experience:* in this introductory chapter you have looked at your own behaviour and character, and thought about the influence of others upon you. An understanding of self can improve understanding and tolerance of the behaviour of others.

INTRODUCTORY ASSIGNMENT

Link: production and employment in the economy

This introductory assignment provides an opportunity to practise some of the skills you will be called upon to use in this book: carrying out investigations and research, conducting a survey and writing a report based on the results of that survey. It also enables you to look at how individuals benefit from work and what it is about work that they miss when they have none. In Chapter 6 you will be asked to refer back to the results of this introductory assignment.

Task

Select a minimum of five people who are unemployed or who have been unemployed at some time during their working lives. In order to obtain a balanced sample you should aim to include at least one person from each of the following age groups:

- 16–19
- 20–29
- 30–39
- 40–49
- 50–59

Find out from each person:

- *Why she/he wants/wanted to work.* Most people will name money first, so try to find out their other reasons.
- *How she/he feels/felt about being unemployed.* Possible answers may include the time to do other things. Alternatively those questioned may have found it difficult to fill their time and therefore experienced boredom.
- *What she/he misses/missed about work.* The answers here (apart from money) may include loss of social opportunity, achievement, satisfaction.

You will find it helpful to design your questions in the form of a questionnaire. This will ensure that you ask each person identical questions. It will also provide a record of their answers in a form suitable for comparison.

As this is only a small survey, it is suggested that you prepare your list of questions and then conduct an interview with each person separately to obtain their answers.

When you have completed your analysis, write a brief report on the results you have obtained and the conclusions you have drawn from them.

Guidelines to this Assignment

Questionnaire

First, decide exactly what information you need to fulfil the task you have been set.

Second, design questions to obtain that information. Phrase your questions in such a way that:

- They are easily understood.
- They are capable of one meaning only (the one you intended) and cannot be interpreted in any other way.
- They provide answers that are easy to analyse (a question that can be answered Yes or No is far easier to deal with and compare than one that requires a lengthy answer that is fundamentally different for each person who completes your questionnaire).

Core skill: information technology

A word-processed and well-set-out questionnaire will help when conducting the survey and also when you analyse the results.

Finally on completion of the survey you will need to analyse the replies you have received. It will be useful to draw up a chart, based on your questions, so that you can transfer the answers from all the questionnaires on to the chart to identify quickly any obvious similarities or differences in the responses (see above about simple answers!)

Core skill: application of number

From your chart, you will also be able to work out the percentages of like answers, and so on.

Report Writing

Core skill: communication

For a short report, such as the one asked for here, you will need:

- The title or subject of the report.
- The name of the person completing the report.
- Introduction:

  - the task you were asked to carry out (terms of reference);
  - how you carried it out (procedure).

- Findings: what you have found out (essentially a description of your analysis of the questionnaire replies).
- Conclusions: what you consider the results and your analysis reveal about people's feelings when they want to work but can not find a job.
- Extra information such as your questionnaires, tables of results and so on can be at the end of your report as appendices.

Reports should be written in the third person, for example 'A report was requested . . .' not 'I was asked to do a report . . .'

PART A INVESTIGATING MANAGEMENT STYLES

2 DEVELOPMENT OF MANAGEMENT

2.1 THE STUDY OF MANAGEMENT

This chapter concentrates on the role of management within the organisation and the different styles of management that can be found. Good management is recognised as an important factor in the success of any business but the training of managers is still a relatively recent idea – most major studies of management have taken place during the twentieth century. The expansion of qualifications for managers is very recent indeed, and books on how to manage now appear on every bookstall, alongside books on how to keep fit, surf the Internet or repair your car.

2.2 PORTFOLIO ASSIGNMENT

The portfolio assignment at the end of Part A (Chapters 2–5) uses case studies to provide a range of situations for the investigation of management styles. Students who have access to business organisations through their work or work experience may also wish to use these in their investigation.

2.3 WORKING WITH CASE STUDIES

**CASE 3
MATTHEW**

Matthew is the owner and manager of a small building and joinery firm. The workforce consists of himself, his wife, his brother and his son. The work they undertake includes small-scale extensions and conversions, fitted furniture and kitchens, garages and carports, fences and gates, and so on.

Matthew has just taken on an urgent job to make and install some fitted wardrobes. He has also started to build a brick garage for another customer but

bad weather keeps stopping this work, and he has been contracted to make and
erect some fencing around the car park at a local factory.

The above is an example of a short case study (the questions on it
appear in Activity 2.2). Case studies based on real or simulated events
are often used in business training to create a situation reflecting the
real world. They provide an opportunity not only for the application
of learning and knowledge but also for practice in dealing with
business problems. Students are asked to study the case and then to
interpret what has happened or to analyse the problems presented
and suggest possible solutions or courses of action.

Suggested Guidelines for Tackling Case Studies

First, read the case study quickly in order to obtain an overall picture
of the situation.

Second, write down in two or three sentences what the case study is
about.

Third, read the case study again, but slowly and carefully this time.
Mark or make a list of important points or points you think may be
of relevance.

For example in the above case study the points you may note are:

- The nature of the organisation: type of business.
- What the organisation does: the type of work it handles.
- Organisation structure and staffing.
- The jobs the firm has 'in hand' at the moment.
- Any particular points about each of those jobs you feel might
  become relevant.
- Any possible problems you can identify or foresee.

Fourth, re-examine the information you have been given and
consider it critically. For example:

- What is factual?
- What is opinion?
- What is important (some points that appear irrelevant may give
  important 'clues')?
- Have any assumptions been made?
- Are there any signs of prejudice or bias in the way the
  information is presented?

By now you should have a clear understanding of the case study. It is
recommended that you should now, and not before, read the

questions you are asked to answer in connection with the study – if you read them before this point it is quite likely that you will read the case study *with only the questions in mind*. This often means that important points are missed or you see an 'obvious' answer and miss other possibilities.

Problem Solving Case Studies

If you are asked problem-solving questions, now is the time to identify and analyse the problems raised in the case study and determine the causes of the problems. Here it is important to distinguish between problems and symptoms! For example, if you have a sore throat you may take some form of medication that claims to soothe sore throats. However the sore throat may actually be a symptom of another illness. The medication therefore soothes the sore throat but does not deal with the illness causing it. Similarly in your case study, what appears to be a problem may in fact only be a symptom of a larger problem. It is important that you investigate this.

Having defined the problems you should now consider alternative ways of dealing with or solving them. In most business case studies there will be alternative ways of solving problems and you will be asked to recommend one. To do this you should outline each of your alternatives and look at what is likely to happen as a result of each solution you have suggested. This will then provide reasons on which to base your recommendation and justify your choice.

A word of warning: information in case studies is of necessity limited, and you cannot ask for more information when you feel it is lacking – you should base your analysis *on the information you are given*. If you feel you have to make an assumption about information not provided in the case study, you must make it clear that you are making an assumption and your reasons for doing so.

2.4 WHAT IS A MANAGER?

A manager can be described as a person who conducts a business or part of a business operation.

By the mid-eighteenth century, changes in agriculture meant that fewer land workers were needed. New technologies (such as steam power) and inventions (for example in connection with textiles and pottery) enabled new methods of manufacture to be introduced. The

Link: roles and responsibilities of supervisors

development of the coal and iron industry and the building of canals and railways provided a boost to production and trade. Workers who could no longer find work on the land had to move to towns and work in factories built and owned by the new entrepreneurs – those with enough capital to set up and run their own businesses. Production was changing from reliance on skilled craftsmen and women to mechanised unskilled work. As the size of businesses increased the need arose for some workers/employees to assist the owner to manage the work and the workers, heralding the development of supervisors and managerial roles. As the managerial work role expanded, so did the study of what managers did and how they did it. The theories of management that we shall examine reflect the development of work organisations from the late nineteenth century.

2.5   WHAT IS THEORY?

What do we mean here by a theory and how do theories originate? In some cases an individual working as a manager would put together, from his own experience, his ideas of what his tasks were and how he felt the manager's role should be undertaken. (At this stage managers are referred to as 'he' because in most cases they were men!) Some writers on the subject were not managers themselves but academics, usually working in the universities. They went out and investigated the work of managers in a number of organisations and then drew conclusions from their findings. The published work of these people form the basis of management theory. Today's managers learn and study the theories in order to benefit from the work and research of others, and as a result to play their role more effectively. Research into management is still carried out and writers such as Charles Handy, Peter Drucker and John Harvey-Jones are putting forward new ideas they have obtained from their investigation of and experience as managers. Businesses in the 1990s are in many ways different from those of the 1970s. They operate in a more rapidly changing environment, technology continues to develop, the expectations of workers are different, and greater flexibility and skills are needed. Consequently the way in which a manager manages has had to change too – and new theories of management are resulting.

ACTIVITY 2.1   Investigate the three presentday writers named above (Charles Handy, Peter Drucker and John Harvey-Jones). You should try to find out:

1. Their background (academics, practitioners/managers, or perhaps a combination of both).
2. Their careers and the types of work they have done.
3. The titles of books they have written and the particular areas of management about which they have written.

Core skill: communication

(Suggestion: try *Who's Who*, or extract any information the authors provide about themselves in their books.)

2.6 MANAGEMENT THEORY: THE CLASSICAL APPROACH

Henri Fayol

One of the earliest writers about management was *Henri Fayol* (1841–1925), a Frenchman. He started work as a mining engineer and stayed with the same company for most of his working life, retiring in his seventies. During that time he worked his way up to become managing director and turned a poorly performing company into a very successful one.

In 1916 Fayol wrote a book outlining his ideas about management. He said that a manager had to carry out five activities:

- *Forecasting and planning*: studying what is likely to happen in the future, considering what needs to be done, and making plans to meet those needs.
- *Organising*: deciding what has to be done to carry out those plans, arranging for appropriate resources (such as people and materials) to be available and operating in such a way as to meet the timetable for putting the plans into operation.
- *Commanding*: ensuring that the activities are carried out and that the best levels of activity are sustained throughout.
- *Coordinating*: drawing together all the parts and activities involved so that they are achieved in cooperation and fit together smoothly, like the pieces of a jigsaw.
- *Controlling*: making sure that what is taking place is in accordance with the plan and is being done correctly and to the required standard, that deadlines are being met and costs not exceeded.

ACTIVITY 2.2   Read Case 3, at the start of this chapter (Matthew). Describe how Matthew is carrying out Fayol's five activities in his role as manager of his firm.

Max Weber

Another writer of the same period as Fayol was *Max Weber* (1864–1920). He was not a manager himself, but was on the academic staff of a German university. He studied organisations in terms of their structure and those who had authority within that structure. Weber said that the type of authority the superior had over the subordinate that the subordinate would accept fell into one of three categories: traditional, charismatic or rational–legal.

- *Traditional authority* was based on accepted custom and practice. This sort of authority would come from a religious leader or a monarch.
- *Charismatic authority* arose out of the personality or 'charisma' of the leader. People did what he or she said simply because of the force of his or her personality, because they appeared to believe that person had very special qualities.
- *Rational–legal authority* comes from the position held by the individual. An organisation has particular objectives and sets up rules and procedures in order to create a structure that can fulfil those objectives. The position in question is part of that structure and as such extends authority over those answerable to the holder of that position. In this instance the authority follows from the position rather than the individual who occupies the position at any one time. The type of organisation described above as giving rise to rational–legal authority was called by Weber a *bureaucracy*.

Weber examined three aspects of bureacracy:

- *Rank*: the hierarchy of the organisation – who was answerable to whom.
- *Roles*: the functions of each position within the hierarchy and the skills needed for that position.
- *Rules*: those dictates that governed what was done and how it was done.

A bureaucratic organisation would have all matters relating to these three aspects precisely laid down in writing, so that they were orderly, clear and regulated.

ACTIVITY 2.3   Discuss what we mean today by a 'bureaucracy'. How is it different from Weber's meaning of bureaucracy?

F. W. Taylor

So far we have looked at the nature of management (Fayol) and the structure and organisation of businesses (Weber). A third theorist, F. W. Taylor (1856–1915), like Fayol, was a manager and developed his ideas from his own experience of trying to increase efficiency (and therefore profits) in the companies in which he worked in America. He began as an engineering apprentice and progressed into management, eventually publishing his ideas.

Taylor recommended what he called *scientific management*. From his experience on the shop floor he believed there were ways to improve production levels:

- Break down every aspect of the job into discrete (individual) tasks and find the quickest method of doing each task.
- Train every worker so that each did the task assigned in a prescribed way in the time set.
- Organise the shop floor so that each worker could concentrate solely on his task. Managers would take on all other responsibilities, their roles also governed by this 'scientific' approach, and see the worker followed the set method of working.

Taylor's ideas now form the basis of what is called *work study* – analysis of the content of a job, the time taken to do each part of it and the development of the most efficient (cost-effective) way of carrying it out.

Scientific management is generally associated with production methods, and particularly that of mass production. The tendency in scientific management was to regard people in the same way as machinery. Little thought was given to the worker as an individual. Each worker concentrated on a small part of the operation, and the methods of working rarely gave the individual the opportunity to see how his task fitted into the whole. There was little personal involvement or commitment, or encouragement to be part of a workgroup.

Attention to the worker was taken up by proponents of the human relations school of thought.

ACTIVITY 2.4   What do you think are the advantages and disadvantages for the worker of Taylor's scientific management approach to production?

2.7   MANAGEMENT THEORY: THE HUMAN RELATIONS APPROACH

Elton Mayo and the Hawthorne Studies

Elton Mayo (1880–1949) was an Australian who went to live in America. He trained as a psychologist and became professor of industrial research at Harvard University. Between 1927 and 1932 Professor Mayo was asked to carry out a series of studies at the Hawthorne plant of the Western Electric Company.

In one of the studies – the relay assembly test-room experiment – researchers investigated the effect working conditions had on productivity. For example changes to the length and time of the lunch break were made, and the number and length of rest pauses altered. Each time the prospective change was first discussed with the workers, then the change was introduced and the productivity level measured. Strangely, productivity increased when conditions were made worse as well as when they were made better. The workers' performance was improving *as a result of the attention they were receiving* rather than as a result of the changes in conditions.

In another study – of a bank wiring observation room – the behaviour of a particular group of workers was monitored to see how the group behaved (this is looked at in more detail in Chapter 9). Other studies involved interviews being carried out throughout the plant, another the introduction of personnel counselling.

From the findings obtained from the Hawthorne Studies, the following main conclusions were drawn:

- Being part of a group was important to workers.
- Groups developed group attitudes and set their own rules, and members of a group usually stuck to the rules and responded to the group's influence.
- Relationships were very important and affected the attitudes of workers, particularly the relationship between supervisor and worker.

The scientific management theorists had not thought about the workers, how they felt and behaved. Rather they had looked at the production process or the structure of the organisation. Now interest developed in the behaviour of the people in the organisation and the effect of this on production and the organisation.

Abraham Maslow and Frederick Herzberg each developed theories about the needs of individuals and how these affected the individual's motivation. We shall look at these particular theories in more detail in Chapter 7.

ACTIVITY 2.5   Discuss reasons why, in the relay assembly test room experiment, the workers' performance improved because of the attention they were receiving. What can managers learn from this experiment?

McGregor's Theory X and Theory Y

Douglas McGregor (1901–1964), an American social scientist, developed what he called *Theory X and Theory Y*. He maintained that managers had two different views of workers:

- Theory X managers believed workers disliked work and avoided it if possible, that they were lazy, did not want responsibility and preferred someone else to tell them what to do. As a result these managers felt that workers had to be controlled, forced to work, and threatened with punishment if they did not.
- Theory Y managers believed that workers liked work and saw it as a natural thing to do. In the right conditions workers would accept and even seek responsibility. They could be creative and committed to the organisation's objectives.

The view a manager held would obviously influence the way he treated the workers – and the way the workers responded!

ACTIVITY 2.6   Discuss in groups how do you think workers would respond to

- A Theory X manager
- A Theory Y manager

Core skill:
communication

Can you give examples to support your views, drawing on your own experience as an employee or a student?

2.8   MANAGEMENT THEORY: THE SYSTEMS APPROACH

From the 1950s onwards, researchers brought together the ideas of the classical and human relations theories to develop what was called the *systems approach*. The principles behind the systems approach were originated by scientists working in Massachusetts during the Second World War and were influenced by the work of biologists on natural systems.

A system is made up of interrelated parts and consists of:

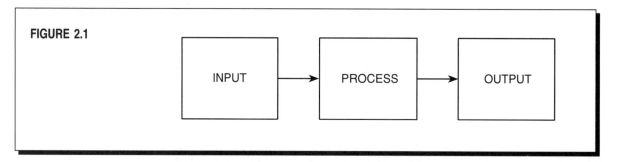

FIGURE 2.1

For example, in a computer system data is fed into the computer, the computer then carries out the appropriate processes and prints out the information required. In the sales department of an organisation, an order is received (input), dealt with by various people within the organisation (process) and the goods and an invoice are sent out (output).

Usually systems are considered to be closed or open. In a *closed system*, without outside help the system automatically adjusts itself to meet changing circumstances. For example, in a central heating system with thermostatic control the heating is automatically turned off when a certain temperature is reached. When the temperature drops the heating is automatically switched on again. An *open system* will interrelate constantly with events, circumstances and other systems around it. An open system such as a modern business organisation will therefore be in a continual state of change as it adjusts and adapts to, for example, the current economic environment, the activities of its competitors, the skills of the workforce, new technology, management decisions and so on.

Systems theory maintains that you cannot look at one part of a system in isolation because it will be influenced by all the things happening in other parts of the system. So, for example, the work of the sales department of an organisation will be affected by the production levels of the production department, the advertising campaign developed by marketing, how rapidly the finance department pays travel expenses (of the sales representatives), and so on. In addition the sales department will be affected not only by what is happening *inside* the organisation, but also by *outside* events – a strike at the TV company where the advertising is scheduled to appear, for example!

Link: people in business organisations (intermediate)

CASE 4 DRIVING

Learning to drive a car can be very alarming at first – there are so many things to do at the same time and so many things to think about. Yet a driver learns to do this and to coordinate all the necessary actions. Look at the diagram below, which draws together some of the factors that might be involved in driving a car (you can probably add to it).

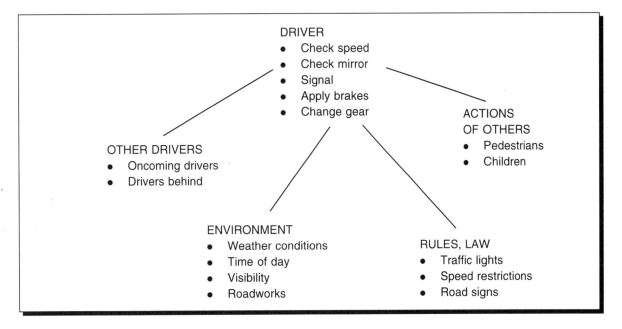

In case 4 driving a car involves (at least):

- Your own actions
- Actions of others
- The environment
- Rules, law

In a similar way, a business exists within a complexity of overlapping systems. A variety of interrelating activities are taking place inside the organisation, but the business is also affected by events and activities that take place outside it.

ACTIVITY 2.7   In the blank spaces in the diagrams below, write down the factors that affect the way a business operates:

(a)   Internal factors affecting the business

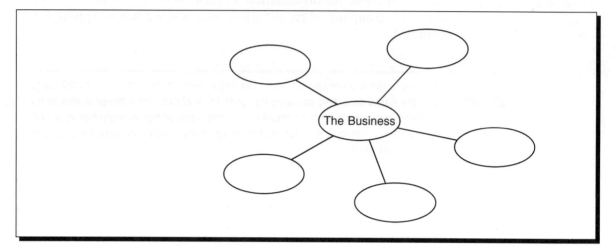

(b)   External factors affecting the business

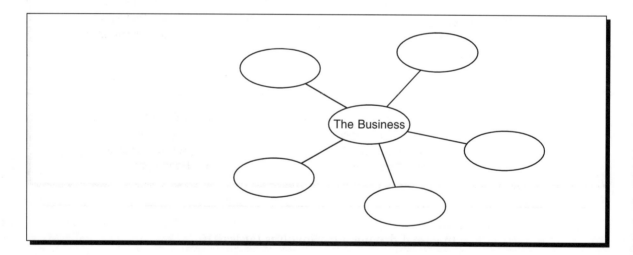

Trist and Bamforth

An example of research based on the systems approach is the one on coalmining that Trist and Bamforth of the Tavistock Institute for Human Relations in London conducted in the 1940s.

The researchers first studied the old system of excavating coal – the short wall method, whereby the miners worked in small groups, each group working independently at separate small coal faces. When a mechanised coal cutter was introduced that operated on one large coal face, the miners began to work in one large group per shift. This was called the long wall method and the workers were organised to make maximum use of the new equipment. Trist and Bamforth discovered that this new method of working was producing a number of problems – more disagreements between workers, a higher accident rate, increased absenteeism. They recommended a change in how each shift was organised. The new equipment was still used, but the workers were reorganised into small groups. The result was increased productivity, less absenteeism and fewer accidents. Trist and Bamforth had not studied the work system and the human system in isolation from each other, but had looked at the two together. Consequently they were able to devise a method of working that both satisfied the workers' social needs and made best use of the new equipment.

2.9 MANAGEMENT THEORY: CONTINGENCY THEORY

The systems approach examined factors both inside and outside the organisation that influenced how the organisation performed. From this, during the 1960s *contingency theory* was developed. This identified four major areas that affect an organisation:

- The people in it.
- The technology it uses.
- The formal structure of the organisation.
- Outside factors – the environment in which the organisation operates.

These four factors were seen as forming the basis of how an organisation functioned and how it was being or should be managed. Contingency theory suggested that there was no right way to manage a business. The best way was individual to a particular organisation and depended on the way the four factors were combined.

ACTIVITY 2.8   Select one of the following:

- Your school
- Your college
- Your place of work

1. Draw up a chart with the four factors of contingency theory placed at the top of four columns.
2. In each column write a brief description of how that particular factor is made up. For example in a school the people would include students, teachers, governors, administrative staff, catering staff, cleaning and maintenance staff and so on. The outside factors affecting a school would include such things as government policy, funding and other schools in the area.
3. When you have completed the chart, place your four factors in order of importance, as you see it.

Core skill:
communication

4. Discuss your results with those of others who have selected the same type of organisation.

2.10   SUMMARY

Theories of management

Classical approach:

Fayol, the five activities of management:

- Forecasting and planning
- Organising
- Commanding
- Co-ordinating
- Controlling

Weber, bureaucracy, structure and organisation:

- Rank
- Roles
- Rules

Taylor, scientific management.

Human relations approach:

Elton Mayo and the Hawthorne Studies:

- Importance of groups and the relationship between workers and supervisors.

McGregor, Theory X and Theory Y.

Systems approach:

- Open and closed systems.
- Interrelating and overlapping systems.
- Trist and Bamforth, coal excavation.

Contingency theory:

The four factors:

- People
- Technology
- Structure
- Environment.

3 MANAGEMENT STYLES

3.1 WHAT IS MANAGEMENT STYLE?

We have looked at the growth of management theory and seen how ideas about management have developed from the different ways of looking at a business organisation, that is:

- The production methods it uses.
- The people in it.
- Its use of technology and equipment.
- What is happening in different parts of the organisation and their effect on each other.
- Events happening outside the organisation that influence the organisation.

We now move on to look at the managers themselves.

Any student at school or college knows that no two teachers teach in the same way. Each has his or her own method of teaching and working with students – his or her own *style*. At work, too, you will notice the different ways in which managers deal with their role. Workers often find that it takes time to become used to a new supervisor's way of working, not necessarily because it is better or worse than the predecessor's way, but simply because it is different.

The way in which a manager manages may depend upon two factors:

- The style of management adopted by the manager.
- The personal qualities and temperament of the manager.

Obviously these are closely related in that personal characteristics tend to affect the style in which managers carry out their duties.

3.2 STYLES OF MANAGEMENT

Usually management style falls into in one of three categories:

- Autocratic or authoritarian
- Democratic
- *Laissez-faire.*

The *autocratic* or *authoritarian* manager expects to make all decisions him or herself, decides on how goals will be achieved, allocates tasks and expects workers to carry out his or her instructions. This manager would not consult workers or involve them in decision making or target setting. Information and communication tend to flow in one direction – from the manager to the workers. Rewards and punishments are controlled by the manager.

In the *democratic* style the manager is part of a group and encourages the members to take part in decision making and to share tasks and responsibilities. The key words in the democratic style are participation, involvement and cooperation. There is a constant exchange of ideas and information, and good communication is important.

The *laissez-faire* manager stands back from the group, ready to step in if needed, but otherwise – if the group members are working well – allowing them to continue without unnecessarily involving him or herself. The *laissez-faire* manager does not ignore his or her responsibilities or shirk decision making. However she or he neither constantly interferes or instructs, nor becomes part of the group in the way the democratic manager does. The *laissez-faire* manager is more inclined to monitor the group's performance from a distance, but is willing to help or step in if necessary or if she or he is asked.

An organisation may demonstrate more than one management style. For example the overall style, set perhaps by the chairman or managing director, may be autocratic but an individual manager may adopt a democratic approach within his or her section or department. In the presentday business environment there is greater awareness that a particular style may be appropriate to that organisation or in those circumstances.

One word that crops up frequently when discussing management and managers is leadership. Sometimes we talk of managers and leaders as though they are the same thing, but there are important differences. Ultimately a manager is responsible for getting things done. Management is concerned with the organisation of activities and people in order to complete tasks and achieve objectives. An important part of the manager's role is drawing together – integrating – a number of activities. In contrast leadership arises directly out of relationships with people. A leader is an individual whom others will follow. It is the personality and personal qualities of the leader that attract loyalty. Usually a leader goes out in front (leads) and sets an example, inspiring and guiding others so that they will wish to follow.

Imagine a mountaineering expedition. A 'manager' would arrange finances and sponsorship if appropriate, organise supplies, select people with the right qualities and allocate their roles and duties, draw up route plans, select camp sites and so on. It would however be the 'leader' who would hold the team together, unite them in the dream of what they are to achieve, keep them going when things get tough or disaster strikes. From this example it becomes apparent that the person in charge of the expedition would need to be both a manager and a leader. A good leader will have management abilities just as a good manager will have leadership qualities. (We shall look at leadership qualities in more detail in Chapter 4.)

The following case describes an actual company that set out to change its management style to one that it was believed would improve relationships and get the best out of people.

CASE 5
NUCLEAR ELECTRIC

'Culture change has been a fact of life for Nuclear Electric since 1991. Management development has taken place amid a raft of change programmes including teamworking and quality improvement initiatives. "The role of managers in the business has moved away from a directional style to a less bureaucratic, more open one," says management training manager Paul Rann.

"The change from management to leadership roles requires senior managers to operate in a coaching, facilitating way."

Rann has instigated a system of management competencies which include open communication, people development and coaching. He also decided to buy in the expertise of Performance Consultants, in the person of former Olympic hurdler David Hemery, to help senior managers move from a chiefly technical to a more people-orientated role.

"The messages Hemery brought with him were extremely powerful," says Rann. "They were about how managers through a questioning, listening style can get the best out of people."

"It challenged basic assumptions, too, such as that this generation of managers can only be as good as the last generation."

Eighty per cent of Nuclear Electric's senior managers have now been through the programme. "Measuring results is very difficult," says Rann. "But the benefits are obvious. We are talking about highly qualified, very bright technicians who don't always take too well to soft-skill management philosophies. But they have universally embraced the coaching style."

"Employees give anecdotal feedback, that senior managers are now much more inclined to listen, question, agree targets."

Rann's next move is to train in-house facilitators so the coaching techniques can be cascaded right through the organisation – but that means first finding people within the line who possess the right qualities.

"We are scouring the business to find individuals whose behaviour and style mirrors the coaching philosophy."'
(Reproduced with the kind permission of *Personnel Today* from 'Training – A Personnel Today Supplement', June 1995. © *Personnel Today*.)

ACTIVITY 3.1   Read Case 5, then answer the following questions.

1.   Describe the styles of management before and after the change at Nuclear Electric.
2.   What were the skills in which managers were trained in order to bring about the change of style?
3.   What results were reported by employees?
4.   Why do you think the new management style is more appropriate for the 1990s?

3.3   WHAT AFFECTS THE OVERALL MANAGEMENT STYLE?

The Organisation and the Nature of its Business

Soldiers are trained to fight as part of a team. The activities of an army in battle must be coordinated – success and the safety of others (colleagues and civilians) depend upon it. Democratic discussion is not appropriate nor in general is it an environment in which you can 'do your own thing'. To meet the overall objective, orders must be followed precisely and without question, rules and procedures are vital. An army is therefore a very authoritarian organisation. In contrast a marketing project team aiming to come up with a new brand name and image will operate in an entirely different way. Here creativity is the essential objective. Ideas must be generated, and the members must work together, bounce their thoughts off each other and spark each other's imagination.

Link: business organisations and systems

ACTIVITY 3.2   Consider each of the following organisations. Then, in groups, suggest aspects of each organisation that could influence its management style.

- Hospital
- Fashion house

- School
- Pharmaceutical manufacturer
- Solicitor

The Organisation's Objectives and its Environment

Link: business in the economy

The business organisation wants to stay in business, to maintain and increase its share of the market. How hard it has to work to meet its objectives often depends upon the environment in which it operates. In the 1970s, when the microcomputer industry was relatively new, businesses developing the new technology tended to revolve around a small group of highly skilled, creative people, or in some cases a single individual. The industry is now intensively competitive, a market in which the objective in order to survive is to keep ahead of rival firms.

Link: production and employment in the economy

Those who are employed in the industry today work in an environment where there is great pressure for the rapid development of new and improved software and hardware systems – the winner will be the firm that launches its product first.

Link: business organisations and employment (intermediate)

This background demands a management style that is very different from the enthusiastic leadership of the 1970s. Many of the original manufacturers did not survive – they fitted in with the earlier environment but failed to compete in the latter.

Businesses react primarily to the demands of customer. However, businesses often create the need and sell that to their customers as well as the product. Think of the fashion industry, where each year the designers dictate the new fashions, creating a demand. The same principle is now being applied to how we furnish our homes as fashions for interiors are changing, to what we plant in our gardens, and to the different foods we eat. Occasionally a particular film will create an enthusiasm for all things ethnic or gothic, or a television series for a particular historical period.

The need to be responsive to demand or even to create it is part of the increasing pressure upon businesses to be flexible and capable of handling change. Managers have to become better at adapting their style to the changing environment, as illustrated in Case 5 above, or in providing opportunities for the next generation of managers, as described in Case 14 (Sun Microsystems – Chapter 8).

ACTIVITY 3.3   Describe an example (or find a newspaper or magazine article of one) that illustrates the setting of a fashion or trend.

3.4   WHAT AFFECTS AN INDIVIDUAL MANAGER'S STYLE?

The Organisation

An individual manager is affected by the general *climate and culture* of his or her organisation – the overall style and ethos of the organisation. For example one high street retailer has traditionally been seen by its staff and customers as a benevolent and caring organisation, a certain bank markets itself as the one that listens to the customer, and a major oil company promotes its concern for the environment. Case 11 (Lands' End Direct Merchants UK Ltd – Chapter 8)), and Case 13 (John Lewis Partnership – Chapter 8) illustrate two organisations that share some common objectives in their approach towards staff and customers, but nevertheless possess very individual styles and cultures.

Large public sector organisations, such as local authorities, tend to be bureaucratic as a result of their size, the nature of their operation and their need to be accountable to the public.

ACTIVITY 3.4   Local authorities are 'accountable to the public'.

Link: business organisations and systems

1.   What does this mean?
2.   How does it affect the way in which local authorities operate?
3.   How might this affect the role of an individual manager?
4.   Can you identify other public sector organisations that are similarly accountable?

In an organisation in which the general style is informal and relaxed, a manager will find it difficult to be rigid and authoritarian in the control of staff. Similarly, it would be inappropriate to adopt a casual approach in an organisation that places great importance on rules and procedures.

Managers are also affected by the objectives of the organisation. For example an organisation that wishes to maximise sales and increase its share of the market will adopt a different approach from an organisation that sets out to cut costs and increase its efficiency. An organisation that sets both those objectives may well experience serious conflicts of style in different areas and between departments, such as marketing and finance.

ACTIVITY 3.5 Give examples of conflicts that could arise between the marketing manager and the finance manager of an organisation that sets both the above objectives.

The Task

The nature of the immediate task to be carried out, what it involves, how long it will take and who is to do it are all factors that influence the way in which a manager carries out his role. For example a large, urgent order on production may require supervisors to push their production workers extra hard to meet a delivery date. A sales office manager of an agricultural machinery firm may find that at certain times of year she or he has to ensure that the large number of panic calls from farmers needing their equipment repaired urgently are dealt with promptly. At other times of the year interest has to be fostered when the telephones are quiet and perhaps more boring routine duties must be carried out.

CASE 6 SITUATIONS VACANT **Production Manager**: Will manage 120-strong workforce on shifts in a fast, continuous production environment. Must provide evidence of ability to achieve increases in production levels while keeping to strict cost and quality controls.

Training Manager: Will be responsible for the training department (two training officers and three administrative/clerical staff) and all aspects of training provision. In particular, will be required to set up and monitor NVQ programmes over a range of specialist areas, provide courses as needed to meet new legislation and health and safety requirements, and develop teamwork training across the organisation.

Business Development Manager: Will head small team to consolidate existing customer base and develop new markets for our products, both in the UK and abroad, identifying prospective customers and business opportunities. A proactive role requiring an innovative and dynamic individual.

ACTIVITY 3.6 Case 6 gives brief extracts from advertisements for three different managers. For each manager, from the information you are given:

1. In your own words, describe the major tasks the job involves.
2. Which aspects of the job do you think will affect the management style?

The People

The manager is responsible for the people working under his or her authority, not just to see that they fulfil their duties but also to look after their welfare. She or he must get the best out of these people in order to complete the task effectively. However getting the best out of people involves looking after them. The manager must consider their needs and future prospects, as well as the long-term benefits to the organisation.

CASE 7
THE NEW
MANAGING
DIRECTOR

Rymings is a long-established family-owned pottery business producing quality tableware. Many of the workers have been with the company throughout their working lives and as a result identify closely with the Ryming family, the company and its products. The company has encouraged this 'family' approach.

Toby Ryming took over last year as managing director following his father's retirement. He is keen, enthusiastic and dreams of developing Rymings into a major pottery company. Declining profitability in recent years has not supported his dream. Shortly after taking up his new position, Toby called in a firm of management consultants. The consultants advised that the company should streamline (reduce) its total range of products, simplify its designs, expand its output in each range to improve cost-effectiveness and reduce its prices so that the products would appeal to a wider market.

Toby eagerly pushed through the consultants' proposals although not all his management colleagues were happy with the plans and the speed with which Toby insisted on introducing the changes. There was a feeling that their views and experience were no longer important.

The range has been reduced to four or five designs, which have been simplified so that less time and skill is needed. Workgroups are larger. A quality control system has been introduced to ensure that quality is being maintained even though the quantity produced is much greater.

At first production increased dramatically and Toby was proud of his achievement. However there are now signs that all is not well. A promising young designer has left and an experienced production manager has decided to take early retirement. The personnel officer reports an increasing level of absenteeism and labour turnover is higher than in any previous year. Production levels have started to drop and there has been an increase in the number of items failing to meet quality standards.

ACTIVITY 3.7   Read Case 7 above, then answer the following questions:

1.   What are the changes in management style at Rymings?
2.   Why are the managers and workers unhappy with the change of style?

3.5 SUMMARY

Styles of management:

- autocratic/authoritarian
- democratic
- *laissez-faire*

Influences on management style:

- The organisation and the nature of its business
- The organisation's objectives and its environment

Influences on the individual manager's style:

- The organisation
- The task
- The people

4 ROLE AND RESPONSIBILITIES OF THE MANAGER

4.1 THE ROLE OF THE MANAGER

The essential duties of the manager can be linked to Fayol's activities (Chapter 2):

- planning what needs to be done and how it will be done;
  forecasting and planning
- organising the work to be carried out in the best way possible and by the appropriate people;
  organising
  commanding
- monitoring the work to ensure it has been done and in the correct way.
  coordinating
  controlling

4.2 THE RESPONSIBILITIES

Link: roles and responsibilities of supervisors

Additionally, or as part of all the above, the manager must work with others. She or he has a vital role in communication and motivation. It is through people, getting things done by others, that the manager carries out his or her function.

In general, a manager has two immediate responsibilities:

- The task, and
- The people.

Some managers are said to be task-orientated, that is, they concentrate primarily on getting the task completed with little thought to the concerns and welfare of the workers. Other managers are described as people-orientated. These managers tend to make

45

people their first priority. They concentrate on looking after their workers, motivating them, talking to them and showing concern for their welfare. The ideal manager would see the two aspects as closely linked – getting the task done and done well will be influenced by how effectively the employees work, which in turn is affected by the manager's attitude towards and concern for them.

Action-Centred Leadership

John Adair came from a military background and during the 1970s and 1980s described leadership as balancing three goals or sets of needs. The following are the components of Adair's theory of action-centred leadership:

- The task
- The group
- The individual

The leader is responsible for getting the job done (task needs). In order to do this, she or he must ensure that the group works well and is developed in order to be at its most effective (group needs). In addition she or he must recognise that each individual within the group has his or her own objectives, problems, needs and so on (individual needs), and she or he must take these into account.

John Adair's approach is very important when considering the role and responsibilities of the manager. In the workplace, if a manager fails to give attention to these three needs the individual may not participate fully as a member of the workgroup, which may then be prevented from carrying out the task effectively. Consequently the initial objective of getting the job done may not be met. Failure to give sufficient attention to any one of the three responsibilities will result in problems in the other areas. Giving too much attention to one may result in neglect of the other two. Therefore the manager must balance all three responsibilities.

4.3   WHAT MAKES A GOOD MANAGER?

Ability to Carry Out the Role and Responsibilities

In order to carry out his or her duties the manager needs to be skilled in three areas:

- *Management.* Fayol's list gives an overview of what a manager does: planning, organising, commanding, coordinating and controlling. A manager needs to be able to work out what needs to be done, how and when it is to be done, who is to do it and what resources will be needed. She or he must then set in motion the process of carrying out those decisions and monitor and evaluate the results.

- *Knowledge.* Knowledge of the specific organisation and the business or industry in which she or he works; of business in general and the practice of it (finance, marketing, and so on); and of law relating to business, its operation and procedures, the safety and protection of those who come into contact with it (for example the legal status of the business, the contracts it enters into, health and safety).

- *People.* Managing people is probably the most important aspect of the manager's role. But managing people implies more than simply making sure that workers work. It is the manager's responsibility to get the best out of people and provide the right climate in which to work. The following extract explains why managing people is so important.

Link: mandatory units

Link: business and the law

CASE 8
TAKING RESPONSIBILITY FOR MANAGING PEOPLE

'As the demands on managers seem to change with every new innovation from the introduction of mobile telephones to the spread of computers to every desk in the office, the single duty which remains unchanged is managing people.

In every organization I can think of the main asset is people, yet it is this area of responsibility which many managers choose to ignore. The organization is only as good as the people who work in it and the people who work in it are only as good as they are encouraged to be by their managers.

In any large office a straw poll of who are the good managers and who are the bad, will normally indicate who are the good communicators and who are the bad!

Managing people is about ensuring that staff are aware of what is expected of them, how they can achieve those expectations and the performance criteria against which their success will be measured. The good manager needs to set these out clearly and needs to communicate them to the staff involved.

Clearly defined success criteria will ensure the effectiveness of the organisation if supported by a systematic approach to projects, thorough evaluation of the training needs of each member of staff and empowerment to the appropriate level, supported by regular discussion on progress to date by managers, supervisors and staff.

It is high time all managers, including engineers, accountants, project supervisors, sales managers and indeed everyone in the organization who has responsibility for one or more members of staff, realises that managing people is their function and that they should acknowledge that responsibility as part of their line management duties.'

Peter Fitzpatrick
Chairman of Education
Institute of Administrative Management

(Reproduced with the kind permission of the Institute of Administrative Management from the *British Journal of Administrative Management*, March/April 1996.)

Ability to Lead

A manager ought to be a leader if he or she is to function well as a manager. But not all managers are leaders, nor are all leaders managers. A manager is part of the organisational structure and is working towards the organisation's goals. The manager's authority comes from his or her position within that structure. A leader has influence without necessarily being part of the organisational structure. An informal work group may well have a leader who influences what the group does and how it behaves but is not part of management and may not even be working towards the organisation's goals.

ACTIVITY 4.1

Core skill: communication

Discuss why it can be important for the organisation that all its leaders are managers and all its managers are leaders.

A great deal of research has been carried out into leadership and the question of what makes a good leader. The results have not been conclusive, and no one has been able to come up with a single set of factors which is common to all good leaders. Nonetheless our first question must be: what is a leader?

ACTIVITY 4.2

1. Working in small groups, discuss and agree on a definition of a leader.
2. Agree a list of personal qualities you would expect to be shown by a leader.
3. Compare your list with those produced by other groups. Did you agree on any qualities?

Ideally your group should have reached a definition that reads something like this: *a leader is someone who has the ability to influence others to act together in order to achieve goals.*

The next question is: how do you become a leader? The usual ways are:

- By being appointed (for example by the organisation) or elected (such as by the group).

- By simply emerging as a result of circumstances (by possessing, for example, the particular skill needed at a certain time or in a certain situation).
- By force of personality (the 'born' leader).

Leadership Theories

Trait theories   These are based on the personal qualities or *traits* of the individual and come from the idea that leaders are born, not made. They support the idea that a leader has special qualities or *charisma* (that is, an unusual ability to influence others, special charm, magnetic personality). Unfortunately the many studies of leaders, both famous and not so famous, have not produced a single set of qualities that applies to them all. Consequently, although it is recognised that some people do have special qualities, it is not possible to draw up a list of characteristics that all leaders will have. The ones most commonly mentioned are:

- A level of intelligence that is generally above that of the group.
- The ability to take the initiative and act on it.
- Self-confidence and belief in oneself as a leader.

ACTIVITY 4.3   Write down the names of four people whom you would describe as charismatic leaders (past or present). Compare your list with those of others in your group or class.

Style theories   These are closely related to the management styles described earlier in this book, in particular the authoritarian and democratic styles.

McGregor placed managerial leaders in one of two categories:

- Theory X managers are authoritarian.
- Theory Y managers are democratic.

(Refer back to Chapter 2 if you need to remind yourself about McGregor's Theory X and Y.)

Tannenbaum and Schmidt set up a model showing a continuum of leadership styles. At one extreme is the totally autocratic leader who makes all the decisions and instructs followers. At the other extreme is the democratic leader who encourages followers to participate and involves them in all decision making. In between the two extremes are leaders who allow their followers varying degrees of participation and involvement: the leader who 'tells' others what to do, the leader who 'sells' his or her ideas and plans, the leader who 'consults' the followers and the leader who 'shares' decision making.

Important to leadership style is the degree of concern the leader has for the task and those involved. A leader with great concern for people is more likely to adopt a democratic style. A leader who concentrates on the task will be at the autocratic end of Tannenbaum and Schmidt's continuum.

Contingency theories and situational leadership   Contingency theories suggest that leadership depends upon a combination of factors and that no single style of leadership is suitable for all situations.

In his research Fiedler suggests that effective leadership depends upon the relationship between the leader and the group, the structure of the task and the strength of the leader's position. For example an appropriate combination for successful leadership would be where a leader has sufficient authority to act, where she or he gets on well with the group, and where the task is clearly defined and achievable.

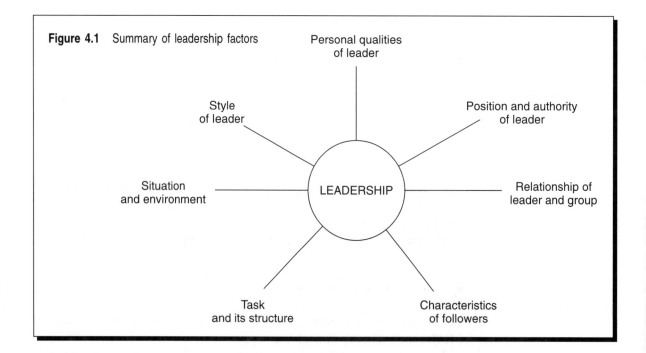

Figure 4.1   Summary of leadership factors

Ability to Motivate

Link: human resources   Managers have a personnel role in connection with those they manage, even when there is a separate personnel department. The manager is responsible for his or her subordinates' safety and protection while at work, for their fair and equitable treatment, for appropriate training and development, and for their overall welfare and wellbeing.

A manager must also be able to get the best out of others. She or he must inspire others to work towards the organisation's goals, and to see their own and the organisation's objectives and success as linked.

ACTIVITY 4.4
1. Name the individuals who have inspired you in some way. (For example you may have had a particular teacher who inspired you to work extra hard, or a supervisor or manager at work who encouraged you to aim for a qualification. Perhaps your own life was helped by someone you read about or saw in a TV programme.)
2. Try to describe what it was about those people or what they did that had the effect on you. (For example interest or belief in you, illustrated courage or determination, imparted enthusiasm.)
3. Discuss and compare your answers to question 2 with other students in your group.
4. Using your information from the above tasks, suggest ways in which managers can motivate their staff and get the best out of them.

When we looked for a definition of leadership we referred to 'influencing' others. A very autocratic leader, one who fits McGregor's Theory X, will control, command and coerce in order to get workers to do what she or he wants. We have also seen that Fayol used the words 'control' and 'command' in his definition of the manager's role. It is important to recognise that a manager must assume authority for getting the job done to the standard set and in the time prescribed.

However when we speak of a manager being able to motivate we are looking at a different aspect of dealing with people. In Activity 4.4 you considered people who had inspired you, that is, made you want to do something and/or do it well. A manager who has the ability to motivate others will have the same effect – workers will feel involved and committed, they will want to do well and take responsibility for their work. The manager has created a climate in which workers work willingly and in which both the organisation's and the individual employee's objectives are satisfied. This is sometimes called a 'win–win' situation, that is, both parties achieve what they want rather than one party achieving his or her objectives at the expense of the other's, a 'win–lose' situation.

In Part B we will examine motivation in greater detail and consider the motivational techniques used by organisations.

Ability to Communicate

We shall look at managers and communication in more depth in Chapter 5. At this point, let us think briefly about what we mean by communication. We tend to think of communication primarily as the process of getting information from Individual A to Individual B. This makes it sound very much a one-way process. In fact good communication must be two-way.

As an example, think about television – does it communicate? It certainly gives out information, but it does that whenever it is switched on, even if there is no-one in the room. Communication can only take place when there is a response, some form of interaction. When you use a computer program that provides questions to which you key in the answers for computer assessment, then you are starting to achieve a form of communication, provided you stay within the limits of the program.

Communication involves interaction, responses from both parties, understanding by both parties. If you speak in English to a French person who knows no English, communication will be limited! Communicating involves listening, understanding and responding. A manager does not just need to be able to speak to employees, she or he must be able to tell when the message has been received and understood, and must be able to listen, to understand their point of view, to recognise their needs. Good communication is yet another important factor in getting the climate right.

Ability to Make Things Happen

In the first half of this century businesses changed slowly in comparison with the speed of change in the later decades. From the 1950s onwards the pace of change increased for a variety of reasons: better education and opportunities led to increased demands for improved lifestyles and material possessions; higher wages brought increasing affluence to a large section of the population; television brought a greater awareness of the world and society in general (to coin a popular phrase, it allowed us to see 'how the other half lives'); technology brought changes to the workplace and the work of the individual. As a result people's expectations were different from those of their parents and grandparents.

Since the 1980s the speed of change has accelerated even more, linked to rapid changes in technology and the changing balance of the world economy. Competition is no longer just the firm down the road or even in another part of the country – it may come from the other side of the world.

All this demands a different approach by managers. A good manager can no longer simply respond to what is happening but must anticipate what will happen in the future and prepare his or her business in advance. In many cases the business now creates the demand for the product rather than making it to meet an existing demand.

In order to do this, managers and workers must be flexible and adaptable to change. A manager must create a work environment in which workers are prepared to meet the new demands made upon them. In general people are reluctant to change. Change requires effort. It often creates fear of failure, as well as fear of the unknown. A manager not only needs to be able to change him or herself but must also be able to create the climate for change and the ability to develop and change in his or her staff. A manager must therefore be *proactive* (that is, able to stimulate activity and change, to make things happen) as well as *reactive* (that is, respond to events).

ACTIVITY 4.5   Learning something new can be exhilarating and exciting. It can also be frightening and difficult, and sometimes tedious and boring.

A student taking a business course might describe the learning experience as follows:

Wordprocessing: very slow and boring at first but when I had learnt where the letters were on the keyboard, I began to enjoy wordprocessing my assignments and was proud of how my work looked when I handed it in.

Financial transactions: I'd not done anything like this before. I found it difficult and confusing – all those forms. Then on work experience I was in a sales office and we used those sales documents all the time. I understood then why the forms were needed. After that it wasn't so bad.

Marketing – product development: I enjoyed this. The product presentation was really interesting to do and I put a lot of time into it.

This student obviously likes practical activities and to see the purpose and usefulness of what is being learnt. Something completely new causes difficulty until the student sees it in a real life business situation.

What about you?

1.   List the areas of knowledge you have gained and the skills you have acquired since starting your course. Then describe in a few words how you felt when you were learning each area of knowledge or skill you have listed.
2.   Compare your list with those drawn up by other members of your class. Are there some areas or skills you all found difficult or exciting? If so, can you identify common reasons for this (for example it was something competely new to you all).

Link: self-development for career planning

3.   Look at your own descriptions. Do the words you have used suggest that you like change and learning new things, or are you reluctant to change and worried about it? If the latter, how do you think you could develop a more positive attitude to change? Can you learn anything from others who are more positive and self-confident?

4.4   SUMMARY

The role of the manager:

- Planning
- Organising
- Monitoring

Responsibilities:

- For the task
- For the people

Abilities of a good manager:

- To carry out the roles and responsibilities
- To lead
- To motivate
- To communicate
- To be proactive

5 MANAGERS AND COMMUNICATION

5.1 THE PROCESS OF COMMUNICATION

Look at Figure 5.1 below. It shows how we put together what we want to say. The initial stages are our thought processes and quite often we are not even conscious of them taking place. Frequently it is only when we begin to learn a foreign language and struggle to translate our thoughts from our native tongue that we come to realise the complexities of language and the perils of choosing the wrong words.

Link: business organisations and systems

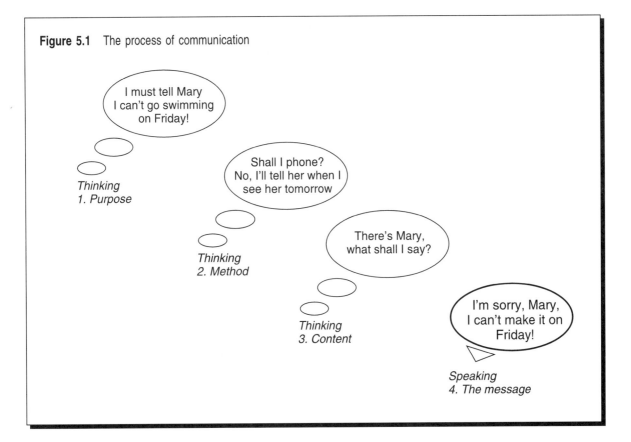

Figure 5.1   The process of communication

First in the process of communication comes the intention or purpose. Then we decide how we will carry it out. Next we formulate in our mind what we will say. Then we actually speak, and deliver the message. But that is only the first part of communication, for at that stage we look for some sign that the person being addressed has heard and understands what has been said. Finally we await a reply, a response to our message, in order to complete the circle of communication.

Figure 5.1 begins to demonstrate the complex structure of communication. Spoken communication involves the mental processing of ideas, selecting the right words to get the message across, listening and trying to understand what the other person is saying, as well as observing gestures and facial expressions to help our interpretation. Of course you may also be 'keeping an eye on the clock' to check that you are not going to miss your bus, or wordprocessing an assignment while talking to a friend!

And the problems do not stop there. The telephone deprives us of the visual, non-verbal signs that help us in direct conversation. In written communication we have to be even more careful of the words we use, their tone and the impression we create, since the recipient of that document has no other signals – visual or aural – to help with the interpretation of the message.

We also learn patterns of behaviour to accompany our communication skills. In conversation we learn not to interrupt, and can recognise when it's our turn to speak. We acquire the correct responses – when to laugh, when to be sympathetic. We develop appropriate social skills for greeting a customer, answering the telephone, dealing with a complaint. We learn to pick up signals and clues from the behaviour of others, to sense an atmosphere when something is wrong, or to judge what is the right way to behave in a particular situation.

Communication is a vital part of our interaction with others, and it is so easy to get it wrong. The ability to communicate well is therefore an important quality for a manager to possess.

5.2   WHY DO MANAGERS NEED TO COMMUNICATE?

Link: business organisations and systems

A manager communicates in the course of his or her work to fulfil three functions:

- *To inform*: it is the manager's role to pass on information. She or he must report to his or her seniors about what is happening in that area of the business. Employees need to be aware of the organisation's objectives and policy. Individuals must be kept informed of progress and advised of changes. Inadequate information may not only lead to mistakes but in some circumstances may also create an atmosphere of mistrust and suspicion.

- *To instruct*: this is the operational part of the manager's work – the process of getting the work done through others. Chapter 3 on management styles showed the different approaches displayed by managers in carrying out this function, and the increasing requirement for managers to be able to adapt to different situations and combinations of factors.

- *To integrate*: this could be termed the maintenance function of communication. The manager must foster the ethos, the general atmosphere and 'feel' of the organisation. She or he must encourage the commitment and involvement of employees, encouraging them to work together and looking after their welfare and development. This aspect of communication is most dependent on a manager's social skills, that is, the ability to get on with people, to talk to them and to listen. Case 5 (Nuclear Electric – Chapter 3) provides a good example of the advantages of this approach but also refers to the reluctance of some managers to use what they see as 'soft-skill management philosophies'.

The importance of communication skills for managers is also clearly illustrated in Case 8 (Taking Responsibility – Chapter 4), where it is suggested that good communicators are usually seen as good managers.

CASE 9
THE SALES MANAGER
(PART 1)

The sales manager arrives at the office. He says 'Good morning' to the receptionist and admires the display of flowers on the reception counter. On the way to his own office he walks through the sales office. As he does so, he chats briefly to individual members of his department:

'Is your cold better?'

'Thank you for the figures you provided, just the information I needed for the managing director.'

'It was a good meeting yesterday, I'd like to talk to you about it later – there are things we need to do.'

'Thank you for getting that message to me, it was important.'

'Had a good holiday? Nice to see you back.'

'I've got a copy of that paper for you.'

ACTIVITY 5.1   Read Case 9, Part 1. What do you think has been achieved through the sales manager's conversations as he arrives?

5.3   HOW DO MANAGERS COMMUNICATE?

Conversation

*Core skills:
communication
Link: business
organisations and
systems*

In general, most communication between manager and worker is verbal and this includes the day-to-day exchange of conversation. As with most conversation, the language and tone adopted, together with the body language used, provide an indication of the relationship between the two parties. Where a relaxed and informal approach is encouraged, this will be reflected in the way the two parties speak, how they address each other and the way in which they sit or stand. In a very formal environment, where the style is more authoritarian or there is less contact between manager and worker, people are more careful in what they say, there is a stiffness about the way they speak as well as in their body language.

A manager who converses little with individual workers will find it more difficult to fulfil the integration function of communication. On the other hand a manager who encourages a too relaxed and familiar approach may have difficulty in carrying out the instruction function.

Written Documents

Memos and Letters

The usual form of correspondence within the organisation is the memorandum, or memo as it is usually called. The letter, with its business headings and formal openings and endings, is only used in particularly formal instances, for example to give notice of redundancy, when it is important that the communication contains the business name and address. For most internal written communications the memo offers a simple, straightforward and to-the-point format. It can be used for a two-line message (some even have space for a reply) or for an internal report.

How fast your memo reaches the recipient, particularly in a large organisation, depends on the speed and efficiency of internal mail system. Just as E-mail (electronic mail) and fax (facsimile) have speeded up the transmission of written documents to and from the outside world, so E-mail can be used within the organisation and between its branches to improve communication and the flow of information.

Reports

A short informal report is quite often written in memo style and in its simplest form may consist of an introduction, the body of the report, a conclusion and recommendations, if appropriate.

A long formal report would not use the memo headings since it would probably have a title page. It would include:

- Title page (title, author, recipient, date)
- Contents page
- Terms of reference
- Procedure
- Findings
- Conclusions
- Recommendations
- Appendices
- References and sources.

Internal Orders

Under this heading is a variety of internal documents that flow between departments to authorise and instruct work to be carried out, goods to be ordered and so on.

For example a job card order would include a job number, details of the job, completion deadlines and the sections or departments in which each part of the job is to be carried out. The order is part of the control system designed to monitor the job and is also used as the basis for costing and invoicing the work. In the sales office an internal sales order form will record the customer's order information (received by post, telephone or fax). Copies of it will go, for example, to stock control, warehouse and accounts to enable the goods to be supplied and the customer charged. Where a computerised order system is in operation, details can be entered on one computer and accessed by or transmitted to the relevant departments. Computerised systems also prepare and print out all appropriate forms and invoices.

A purchase requisition is an internal request for goods to be ordered and is sent to the purchasing department, where terms are negotiated and the goods ordered from the supplier. Maintenance forms will contain requests for walls to be painted, sinks to be unblocked, locks to be replaced and so on.

Interviews

Link: human resources

The verbal interaction that takes place at interviews is usually structured to meet a specific purpose. Interviews for a variety of purposes take place in business, for example:

- *Job or selection interview*: interviews of candidates shortlisted for a vacant position or for promotion.
- *Appraisal interview*: review of employee's performance and progress. Will usually include consideration of any training and development needed and future potential and objectives.
- *Disciplinary interview*: follows employee misconduct. Is conducted in accordance with the organisation's disciplinary procedure.
- *Grievance interview*: arises out of a complaint by the employee. As with disciplinary procedures, organisations must have a formal grievance procedure.
- *Exit interview*: many organisations hold these when an employee has resigned so that they can find out the employee's reasons for leaving. Replacing staff is expensive so an exit interview may reveal problems the organisation can resolve, and thus prevent further loss of staff.

Although some of these interviews may be conducted in what appears to be an informal atmosphere, most have an underlying structure or procedure. In the case of disciplinary and grievance matters the organisation is required by law to have formal procedures and the employee must be informed of these in the statement of employment.

Before conducting an interview the manager should have a plan – of the format of the interview, how long it will take, the approach she or he intends to take, the questions to be asked and the points to be covered. The manager should ensure that she or he is well prepared for the interview and has all the necessary information and documents. Interviews should be structured to allow both parties to speak and give their point of view. Managers should act impartially, fairly and with courtesy, and be prepared to listen. At the end of any interview the manager should sum up what has been said and agreed. The manager should also keep written notes of the interview and a record of what was agreed.

Meetings

Link: operating administrative systems (intermediate)

Meetings have become a familiar activity of the work environment. Some meetings are simply informal gatherings for discussion. A formal meeting is likely to have a regularised composition and procedure (constitution, standing orders).

The chair or chairperson manages the conduct of the meeting following the agenda (the list of items to be discussed, usually sent out in advance) and in accordance with established procedures. The secretary takes minutes, that is, she or he records what happens at the meeting and the decisions taken (the minutes are usually circulated to the participants after the meeting).

Presentations

Presentations by managers may take place when information has to be given to a group of people and/or where that information is more suited to an oral presentation than a written report. This may include such things as changes in health and safety procedures, proposals for buying new equipment, demonstration of equipment or products, and proposed changes to structure or staff.

The information may be presented to, for example, other managers, the board of directors, a department, or all or part of the workforce. The reasons for a verbal presentation may include:

- Subject is complex.
- Demonstration is required.
- Use of video, slides or overhead projector for greater clarification, supporting material, and so on.
- Opportunity for questions to be asked.
- Opportunity for discussion.
- People may not read a written report.
- Everyone can be told at the same time.

In the modern business world there is an expectation that such presentations will be professional and sophisticated – the audience will be used to television and other media. (If you doubt the standard of presentation on television, you only have to watch old TV programmes and advertisements to appreciate the development of skill, technology and style of presentation!) A manager is now expected to give a polished performance. Advanced wordprocessing packages and desk top publishing have increased the quality of handouts. Specially designed software permits the production of professional looking OHP and 35mm slides, including colour and graphics, or alternatively the material can be displayed on computer screen. Software for multimedia systems enables sound and video to be added.

Telecommunications

Modern telecommunications have provided improved facilities for contact between managers and their staff as well as between the organisation and its customers. Mobile phones, radiopagers and teleconferencing are examples of the facilities now available, providing instant contact on site or at meetings across the country.

Computers and Networks

Internal computer networks, computer conferencing, electronic mail systems and the Internet have created new methods of communication both within the organisation and in its contact with the outside world. In some cases employees work from home, communicate with the manager and the organisation by computer, and only go into the office occasionally.

CASE 9 **THE SALES MANAGER** **(PART 2)**	9.00–9.15	Reads post and messages. Sales office manager tells him one of their major customers has just rung in to report a problem with one of the new products. Rings customer to arrange to visit them after lunch.
	9.15–10.15	Meeting with senior staff of department to tell them about yesterday's management meeting and how it affects the department. Discuss how they will meet targets.
	10.15–11.00	Works on computer on figures for next year's departmental budget, to be sent to senior management. Interrupted several times by telephone calls.
	11.00–11.30	Disciplinary interview: persistent lateness of a staff member.
	11.30–12.00	Recommences work on budget and its accompanying report. Interrupted several times by telephone calls.
	12.00–2.00	Weekly meeting over lunch with other heads of department.
	2.15–3.55	Visits the customer with the product complaint. Soothes customer and promises that the problem will be investigated and resolved. On return to the office, speaks on the telephone to the technical manager to arrange for the customer's problem to be dealt with and steps taken to correct the product problem.
	3.55–4.45	Deals with the correspondence and makes a number of telephone calls. Drafts memo to staff advising them of the product problem that has arisen, what is being done about it and procedures for dealing with any further complaints.
	4.45–5.00	Gives a short talk on the work of his department at an induction training session for new staff.
	5.00–5.30	Works on the budget report then decides to take it home to finish.

ACTIVITY 5.2   Read Part 2 of Case 9, then carry out the following tasks:

1.   Describe the different forms of communication the sales manager was involved in during his day.
2.   Write a brief account of your activities for one day at school/college/work. Identify the types of communication you were involved in during that day.

5.4   BARRIERS: WHAT PREVENTS EFFECTIVE COMMUNICATION?

Communication is often hindered because other things get in the way, for example a crackling telephone line, background noise, lack of attention. Let's look at some of the most common problems.

- *Doing two things at once.* Are there frequent interruptions and distractions that prevent full attention being given? For example a meeting is being held in the manager's office and the manager keeps breaking off to answer the telephone.
- *Something on my mind.* Does an individual have personal difficulties or worries or have an illness that is preventing full attention being given to what is said?
- *Putting it together.* Is the appropriate language being used? Too much jargon or too many abbreviations not fully understood by one of the parties can get in the way of understanding.
- *If there's a wrong way to do it* . . . Is the chosen method of communication the best or the most appropriate? For example a particular matter might be better dealt with in an informal chat than a formal letter.
- *Setting the scene.* Is the environment appropriate? Is this the right place in which to take someone to task? Would it be better to find a quiet room where there are no distractions and others cannot hear? Does it matter what you wear for an interview, or for an important meeting with a client?
- *Choosing the right moment.* Is now the sensible time to discuss this? Would it be better to wait until the boss is less angry, less busy?
- *Too busy to listen.* What happens if the manager feels under pressure and does not have time to listen? How will the workers feel if the manager never listens and appears to ignore their problems?

- *I'm right.* What about the person who knows she or he is always right and won't consider another's point of view?
- *Not switched on.* Is the other person actually listening? Is one person so busy thinking of what she or he is going to say next that she or he is not listening to the other?
- *That's not what I want to hear.* People are often very good at shutting out what they do not want to hear, or interpreting what is said so that it fits in with what they want to be said.
- *At cross purposes.* Are the two parties talking about the same thing or do they only *think* they are talking about the same thing? Does each person have expectations of what the other will say and is consequently disappointed when it is not said?

ACTIVITY 5.3 Work in small groups of 2–4 people. Each group should then select one of the barriers to communication described above and create a role play around it in order to demonstrate that particular communication problem.

ACTIVITY 5.4 Give an example from your own experience (at work, college or school) that illustrates at least three of the barriers to communication described above.

Communication Skills and the Manager

The manager's communication skills must include the ability to listen as well as to talk. She or he must be able to judge the appropriateness of time and place, and be able to create a suitable atmosphere and environment in which communication can take place. In particular a manager needs to have an understanding of how people behave and why, in order to be sensitive in his or her dealings with others.

5.5 SUMMARY

The process of communication:

- What it involves
- Related behaviour patterns

Why managers need to communicate with workers:

- To inform

- To instruct
- To integrate

How managers communicate with workers:

- Conversation
- Written documents
- Interviews
- Meetings
- Presentations
- Telecommunications
- Computers

Barriers to communication:

- Distractions
- Personal factors
- Language and method
- Time and place

PORTFOLIO ASSIGNMENT

This assignment is based on Case 5 (Nuclear Electric – Chapter 3) and Case 7 (The New Managing Director – Chapter 3). (If necessary reread the suggested guidelines in Chapter 2, Section 2.3 Working with Case Studies.) Study the two cases carefully, then carry out the following tasks.

1. *Management styles.* Identify and describe the different styles of management illustrated in Case 5 (Nuclear Electric) and Case 7 (The New Managing Director).
2. *Responsibilities of managers.* What are the responsibilities of managers and to what extent were they fulfilled in these two cases?
3. *Managers and communication.*
   - At Nuclear Electric, what was the purpose of the management development programme?
   - What communication skills were developed by the programme?
   - Why is good communication between managers and workers important?

4. *Barriers to communication.*
   - To what extent do you think poor communication led to the problems at Rymings?
   - Write a short informal report for Toby Ryming defining the problems at Rymings and recommending strategies he might adopt in order to resolve them.

PART B INVESTIGATING THE EFFECTS OF MOTIVATION ON PERFORMANCE

6 ATTITUDES TO WORK

6.1 WORK AND THE INDIVIDUAL

At the beginning of this book you undertook some research to find out how people felt about being unemployed. Refer back to your results.

- What were the reasons given for wanting to work?
- What did people miss most about work?
- Did other members of your group or class obtain the same results?
- Would you expect these same factors to be mentioned if you questioned employed people about what is important to them?

To find out, carry out Activity 6.1. Almost certainly, money will again figure prominently in your results. As discussed in Chapter 1, money is a means to an end rather than an end in itself. The end may be what is regarded by the individual either as the *essentials* or as the *additionals* to the life style of that individual. One person may work in order to pay the mortgage, another to fund next year's holiday. In reality most of us aim for a combination of essentials and additionals. We hope to earn enough to cover all our essential needs but have sufficient left over for at least some of the extras we would like.

When you carry out Activity 6.1, it could be useful to find out from those who identify money as a reason for working whether the money earned is intended for necessities, for extras or luxuries, or a combination of both.

(Note: Remember that many people dislike discussing or revealing information about their personal finances, so you will need to treat this question with tact and sensitivity!)

ACTIVITY 6.1   Select five people who are employed and ask them the following:

1.   Give three reasons why you work.
2.   Name three aspects of your present job that you enjoy.

3.   Identify three aspects of your present job that you do not like.

4.   Give three improvements that you believe would make your present job better or more enjoyable.

Core skill:
communication   Chart your answers, but do not write a report or a detailed analysis.

ACTIVITY 6.2   1.   Compare the results with those you obtained from the introductory assignment.

2.   Identify any similarities and any differences.

3.   Discuss your results with those obtained by other members of your group or

Core skill: class.

communication   4.   Again identify any major similarities or differences.

It would be helpful to keep to hand your results from the introductory assignment and your individual and group/class results from Activities 6.1 and 6.2 as we move on to look at the major theories on motivation and work. You will then be able to see if your results match any of the theories. You may find this helpful to your understanding of the theories and their application to the real world of work.

6.2   WHAT IS ATTITUDE?

'I don't like your attitude!' Most of us have heard this at some time. The speaker is usually suggesting that the other party is being rude, unhelpful or uncooperative in some way. This impression may have developed from a variety of signals – a look perhaps, something that has been said or the way in which it has been said, an unwillingness to carry out a task, treating a serious matter with flippancy, arriving late at class without an apology! Attitude is more than behaviour alone. It is usual to describe attitude as having three aspects:

- Behaviour
- Thinking
- Feeling

Behaviour

We looked at behaviour briefly in Chapter 1 and considered the factors that affect it, such as:

- Inherited traits.
- Upbringing.
- Influence of people close to us (family and friends, for example).
- Influence of the society and environment in which we live.
- Experience.

Thinking

The way we think is similarly affected by forces and events around us, such as:

- The culture of the social group or society to which we belong: this can include religious beliefs, morals, ideas about right and wrong, relationships with other social groups, even aspects of status in society as a whole, and so on.
- The standards and ideas fostered in us by our families: again this can include religious and moral beliefs. It can influence, for example, the way we think about education, about work, about how we treat others.
- The ideas and views of people with whom we associate or for whom we have a particular respect.
- The ideas we develop from our own learning and experience.

Feelings

Feelings represent our emotional responses. We talk of relying on what we call 'intuition' or 'a gut reaction'. Our emotional responses often develop from what we have experienced in the past. If we have felt good about something in the past, we will expect to feel good when something similar happens again. But feelings occasioned in one situation may unjustifiably be transferred to similar events in the future. For example a worker who has had a poor relationship with one supervisor may be uncooperative as a defence against all subsequent supervisors.

At times, feelings may prevent us from moving on and progressing. A student who has experienced the panic that takes over when the mind goes completely blank in an examination may subsequently insist that she or he cannot do examinations. Learning how to prepare for examinations and how to manage the examination itself – including how to control the panic – may enable the student to cope with and overcome the fear, and to discover that she or he can be successful in examinations.

ACTIVITY 6.3   1.   Select a subject on which you hold a firm opinion. (For example you may take a strong position on animals for food or protecting the environment.)
2.   Outline the view you hold.
3.   Try to identify the origins of or reasons for your point of view:

- When did you first begin to hold that opinion?
- What caused you to adopt that opinion?
- How much of your opinion is based on evidence and reasoned thinking?
- Which aspects of your opinion are based on your feelings or an emotional response?

(Our reasoned thinking and our feelings are both valid, but it is useful to be able to identify the difference between them and to recognise when we need to provide evidence for our opinion, such as when we are trying to convince others.)

6.3   PROBLEMS WITH ATTITUDES

We all like to think that we are tolerant and fair, that our thinking is reasoned and our feelings are justified. But are they? Is it possible that we have prejudices and biases? Do we recognise our own prejudices and biases as easily as we do those of others?

Perception

Problems usually arise from our *perception*, that is, the way in which we see and interpret what we see. The old saying about beauty being in the eye of the beholder reflects this – what is beautiful to one person may appear very ordinary to another. Witnesses after an accident rarely give identical accounts of what happened. If, for example, the accident involved a pedestrian and a car, witness A – who does not drive – is likely to interpret what she or he saw from a pedestrian's point of view; witness B's interpretation of events might be influenced by his or her knowledge and experience as a car driver. Yet both witnesses are telling the truth *as they believed they saw it*. How many arguments begin with 'But you said . . .' from one party and 'No, I didn't, I said . . .' from the other?
    Perception differences may arise from the following.

Selection

We can be very selective in what we see and hear without realising that we are being selective. We quite often hear only what we want to hear and see only what we want to see! A young child who does not want to go to bed will successfully shut out the sound of a parent saying that it is bedtime. A warning that work is not up to standard or that something is wrong may be disregarded because the individual did not wish to be aware of it and therefore did not mentally register the information. In the first instance the child may be deliberately 'not hearing', in the second the individual is unconsciously shutting out unwanted information because it is unwelcome or painful.

Attribution

Attribution is the process by which we give reasons for particular events. A typical example is when a student is late submitting an assignment. The student may insist, and genuinely believes, that the fault is not his or hers – the assignment would have been in on time but the printer broke down; it is the computer's fault. The tutor sees it differently – the student has not managed the work effectively, but left it to the last minute so that any problems could not be accommodated; it is the student's fault. If the problem happens to us we tend to attribute blame to something outside ourselves – a situation or an event. If the problem happens to someone else we are inclined to say it was that individual's fault, rather than the result of a particular situation.

Sometimes we do not acknowledge in ourselves characteristics that we readily point out in others. Frequently a person who has an aggressive manner accuses others of being aggressive. An individual who is always late may get very angry if she or he is kept waiting by someone else.

Stereotyping

It is always very easy to place people in categories. It allows us to make quick judgements but often means that we fail to check whether our 'judgement' of the individual or the group in which we place that individual is correct. We stereotype others by association of job (for example bankers are dull, pilots are exciting, nurses are kind), by physical appearance (for example small people are bossy, high foreheads denote cleverness), by age and sex (for example the elderly are stuck in their ways, women are intuitive, men are logical), and so on. If we allow ourselves to fall into the trap of stereotying people, we fail to acknowledge their individuality and to see them as real people.

The Halo Effect

This is another form of categorisation. In this case we take a few of the person's qualities and base our judgement of the whole person upon them. For example employee A is always on time for work, is always polite and always looks busy – so employee A must be a good worker. On the other hand employee B never rushes about, always looks relaxed and is less smartly dressed – employee B must be lazy. In fact no real evidence has been provided that confirms employee A is a good worker or employee B is lazy. Certain qualities have been used as a basis from which to jump to a conclusion that is not only unjustified but may in fact get in the way of building up a true assessment of the individual.

ACTIVITY 6.4   Refer back to Activity 6.3. Examine your answers critically and objectively – pretend you are reading what someone else has written!

1.   Can you identify anything in what you have written that may be based on or influenced by prejudice, bias or any other of the perception problems described above?
2.   Now give your answer to Activity 6.3 to another person and ask him or her to carry out the same critical examination!

6.4   CHANGING ATTITUDES

Our attitudes are constantly under attack from what happens to us and from what we see, hear and read. As a result particular attitudes may be modified or even changed completely. For example we may decide on first meeting someone that we do not like him or her for some particular reason ('I don't like southerners', or 'northerners', or a similar prejudice that we hold as a result of some previous experience or influence). As we get to know the person better we find that she or he is not as our previous experience had led us to believe and so we change our attitude towards 'southerners', 'northerners' or whatever in general. If, however, the person behaved just as we had expected, our attitude will be reinforced as we consider we have received confirmation that it was correct – and it will be even harder to change that attitude next time.

Charles Handy, in his book *Understanding Organisations* (1976), suggested that it was easier to get people to change their behaviour than it was to get them to change their attitudes. He also warned that changing someone's behaviour did not necessarily mean that the individual's attitude would change too. Changing attitudes can be a major problem in organisations, particularly when individuals or groups within the organisation have become entrenched in negative attitudes over a period of years. Many organisations now recognise the importance of fostering positive attitudes, of encouraging employees to feel a sense of belonging and of developing the 'feel good factor' at work.

ACTIVITY 6.5 Try to recall a situation in which you tried to change the strongly held point of view of another person.

1. Outline the point of view that person held.
2. What strategies did you use to try to change the other person's opinion?
3. Why do you think it is so difficult to change attitudes?

6.5 WHAT IS MOTIVATION?

Link: individuals and the organisation (intermediate)

Motivation is the force that drives us to do something. It can range from fear (for example fear of punishment if we don't do what we have been told to do) to desire (for example desire for praise because we have done a job well) or reward (for example if we complete a piece of work we can go home early). We have reasons for most of our actions, although often we are not fully aware of our reasons or motives (or prefer not to recognise them).

Good thrillers and detective stories are centred around the study of those who 'have a motive'. Our enjoyment of such stories and television dramas is usually enhanced because we like to pit our wits against the hero or heroine to work out 'who did it'!

In Chapter 3 we considered the importance of a manager's ability to motivate others. If a business is to get as much work as possible out of its workers (that is, the best return for its financial investment in labour) the management must find the most effective ways of motivating or persuading the workers to work hard. Think about the following questions:

- Is money the only or the best motivator?
- Will the same rewards motivate everyone?
- Are different motivators appropriate to different types of work?
- Are there some things at work that actually demotivate individuals, that is, make them less inclined to work hard?
- Is motivation affected by age, circumstances, personality?

In the next module, we shall look at theories of motivation and these may give us some answers.

6.6   PORTFOLIO ASSIGNMENT

The portfolio assignment for Part B (located at the end of Chapter 9) is based upon a survey of a particular organisation and investigates motivation at work. The assignment approaches motivation with three questions:

- What are people's attitudes to work?
- What affects their attitudes?
- What motivators are used for performance and are they appropriate and effective?

You will find it useful to read through the assignment at this stage. You should aim to keep the above questions in mind while you are studying the remaining chapters of Part B and also think about the organisation you might select for your survey. The activities and cases will help you to build up ideas of what you are looking for in your survey and how you might apply the theories to your investigation.

6.7   SUMMARY

Work and the individual:

- Reasons for working

Attitudes:

- Behaviour
- Thinking
- Feeling

Attitude problems:

- Prejudice and bias
- Perception

Changing attitudes:

- The problems for organisations

Motivation:

- The force that drives the individual
- What motivates?

7 FACTORS AFFECTING MOTIVATION

7.1 NEEDS OR CONTENT THEORIES

The needs or content theories are based on the principle that we all have needs, our main objective being the satisfaction of those needs. As a consequence the way we behave is motivated by the needs we are seeking to satisfy.

Maslow: Hierarchy of Needs

Probably the best known theory (certainly the one most often remembered by students) is the Hierarchy of Needs. Abraham Maslow, an American psychologist, developed his Hierarchy of Needs in the 1940s in the course of his work.

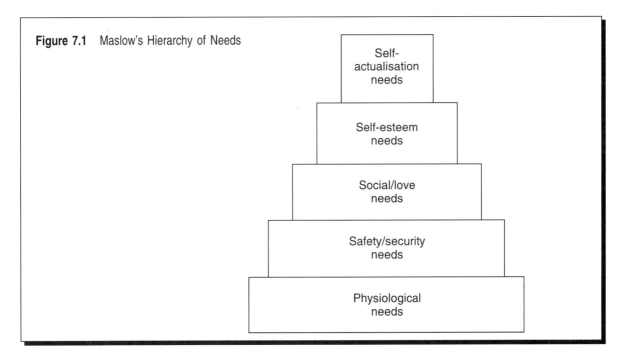

Figure 7.1 Maslow's Hierarchy of Needs

Maslow described the primary needs as physiological. These are based on hunger and thirst and the need for warmth and shelter. A hungry baby usually cries until food is given. Other distractions, such as a toy, will only temporarily draw the baby's attention away from its hunger and stop it crying. A student trying to study in an unheated room on a cold winter's day will find it very difficult to concentrate and to think of anything other than how cold she or he is. The primary needs will therefore obliterate all others, but once these particular needs have been satisfied the individual looks to the next set of needs. These are the second-level needs – the need for a safe environment in which she or he can be free from fear and safe from danger.

Maslow's idea was that our needs are usually progressive – the individual will tend to look to the next need in the hierarchy when the earlier need has been satisfied. The third-level needs relate to the individual's social requirements – the need for contact with others, to be part of a family, to fit into a social group, to have friends and experience relationships with others, to receive and give love and affection.

From the third level the individual progresses to the higher-order needs – steps four and five in the hierarchy. Level four is the need for recognition and respect from others, to be appreciated by others and for the individual to have confidence in him or herself. This is our need for self-esteem and it is usually through the reaction of others towards us that our picture of ourselves develops and we gain confidence.

The fifth and highest level Maslow described as self-actualisation. Here the individual strives for personal fulfilment, to reach his or her or her potential, that is, the goal(s) the individual feels capable of reaching or to which she or he aspires. It is possible that most people never reach complete self-fulfilment, because as one goal is reached a further one may be set. Like a mountaineer, as soon as one mountain has been scaled and we have felt a sense of achievement in that, we look for a more difficult mountain to climb.

Maslow's hierarchy of needs was developed in relation to life in general rather than to work specifically. However much of it can be placed in the context of work and it suggests why we need to work and what we look for in the work we choose to do.

ACTIVITY 7.1   An important point made by Maslow was that once a need had been satisfied it would no longer motivate that person. In small groups, discuss the following questions:

Core skill:
communication

1.   What would this mean if a firm uses only pay as a motivator?
2.   Is there a point at which money would cease to motivate?
3.   Are there individuals who are not motivated by money?

Alderfer: ERG Theory

Alderfer developed his theory of needs in the 1970s. Whereas Maslow listed five sets of needs, Alderfer recognises three:

- Existence needs: the basic needs to exist and survive, for example, food, shelter, safety and security.
- Relatedness needs: the need for social relationships with others, for example friendship and loving relationships, the sense of belonging and fitting in.
- Growth needs: the need to develop our abilities and self-esteem, to feel fulfilled.

Unlike Maslow, Alderfer did not see needs within a hierarchy. Alderfer's view of needs could perhaps be likened to stations in a railway network – we travel between them, stopping at the station (the need) that is important to us at the time and moving on to another when that particular need is either satisfied or frustrated so that we give up on it for the time being.

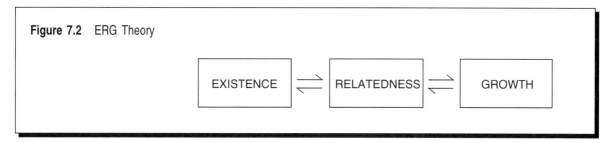

Figure 7.2 ERG Theory

It is necessary to remember that:

- These needs may be satisfied not only at work but also in other areas of people's lives.
- Individuals vary in the level of importance they give to different needs.
- Individuals differ in what they desire in order to satisfy a need.

ACTIVITY 7.2

Core skill: communication

One aspect of Alderfer's studies of needs and motivation suggests that, if existence needs are not met, their importance to the individual become even greater.

In groups, discuss the truth of this with reference to your survey of the unemployed. List the points made by the group, preferably on a flip chart so that it is easily visible, then read the next section on Herzberg's theory on motivation to see if that has any relevance to the points you have made.

Herzberg: Two Factor Theory

In the 1950s Frederick Herzberg carried out a study of over 200 engineers and accountants, asking them which aspects of their jobs made them feel satisfied and which made them dissatisfied.

Herzberg discovered that if the factors that created dissatisfaction were remedied, the worker no longer felt dissatisfied *but did not necessarily feel satisfied.*

To give an example, imagine that the walls of the room in which you are studying are painted in a very dull colour, and are also dirty and scratched. You find it very depressing. One day you arrive to find that the room has been repainted in a colour you really like. It's now a cheerful and pleasant room in which to work. But does that make you enjoy what you are studying? If you did not enjoy the subject before, you are unlikely to gain enjoyment of it simply because the surroundings have improved. A cause of dissatisfaction has been removed but satisfaction is not the result.

Similarly at work there are some things that will make us dissatisfied if they are not to our liking, but it is other factors that actually make us feel satisfied in our jobs. Many people find their work very satisfying even though their surroundings, the conditions in which they work, their pay or their relationships with others are very poor.

Herzberg's point was that the aspects of work that bring satisfaction (Herzberg called them 'motivators') and the aspects that prevent dissatisfaction (called 'hygiene factors' or 'dissatisfiers') are different. At times there may be some overlap between them, often depending upon the individual. For one person pay may be a strong motivator, but for another pay is a dissatisfier if it is below an

Table 7.1   Herzberg's Two Factor Theory

	Hygiene factors (dissatisfiers)	Motivators (satisfiers)
Characteristics:	Lead to dissatisfaction	Lead to satisfaction
	Tend to be concerned with *context/environment* of job	Tend to relate to *content* of job
Factors:	Organisation	Achievement/challenge
	Supervisor/manager	Esteem/recognition
	Surroundings/conditions	Responsibility
	Pay	Actual work
	Relationships with others	Opportunities for
	Status	personal growth and
	Security	advancement

acceptable level. Above that level it plays no part in either satisfaction or dissatisfaction.

Table 7.1 suggests how different aspects of work fall into the two categories.

ACTIVITY 7.3 Examine the two pieces of research you have undertaken (on the employed and unemployed). List the ways in which they are (a) similar and (b) dissimilar to Herzberg's theory.

D. C. McClelland: n-Ach

D. C. McClelland was another American researcher of 'needs' theory. Like Maslow, Alderfer and Herzberg, he identified the *need for achievement* as an important motivator. McClelland felt that this need is influenced particularly by our experiences as children and the background and culture in which we grow up. Children from families in which high standards are set and independence is encouraged are likely to develop a strong need to achieve. This suggests however that we can *learn* the need to achieve (rather than be born with it) and will respond to encouragement and success.

Individuals vary greatly in the strength of their need to achieve. Those with a strong need tend to work hard, and to enjoy and respond to challenge. They like to know how well they are doing and look for evidence of their achievement. They often view the rewards (pay, for example) as an indication that they have succeeded. McClelland identified three needs:

- The need for achievement (n-Ach)
- The need for belonging or affiliation (n-Aff)
- The need for power (n-Pow)

The need to belong closely matches Maslow's social and love needs and Alderfer's relatedness needs. The need for power affects an individual's willingness to assume responsibility and take up a position of authority. McClelland related his investigations to the work environment and in particular to the management role. The strength of each need in an individual can be linked to the type of work in which she or he is most likely to be found – managers show a great need for power; a greater need for affiliation is shown by those for whom relationships are important. Individuals display each of these needs to varying extents, but McClelland saw the need to achieve as the most crucial to work motivation.

ACTIVITY 7.4   Refer to what you have written about yourself in Activities 1.3, 1.10 and 1.11 and consider which of McClelland's three needs is the strongest in your case.

7.2   PROCESS THEORIES

Needs theories looked at the satisfaction of our needs and wants as a basis for motivation. Process theories concentrate on how we perceive or interpret the actual process or means of obtaining what we want. We each approach the satisfaction of our needs in different ways. As a result we are each motivated by different factors or combinations of factors. For the employer this provides additional complexities in that while pay may motivate one worker, another may seek increased job satisfaction, while a third may be attracted by promotion opportunities. Process theories are the result of attempts to interpret or to make patterns of these combinations of motivators. We shall look at three theories:

- Expectancy theory
- Equity theory
- Goal theory

Expectancy Theory

This theory was first put forward and developed in America in the 1960s by Victor Vroom. The basis of expectancy theory is the principle that you put in the amount of effort you think will get you the result or reward you want. In its simplest form, it consists of three stages:

$$EFFORT \quad + \quad PERFORMANCE \quad = \quad REWARD$$

The satisfaction you expect to gain from a particular reward (Vroom calls this the 'valence') will affect the amount of effort you put in. For example if the actual reward is money, the satisfaction you expect to gain will result from what you do with the money rather than the money itself. Expectancy is the individual's anticipation of the likelihood of achieving the reward she or he wants.

However your actual performance will depend not just upon effort. Porter and Lawlor developed expectancy further. They said that other factors are involved in the equation – factors such as ability, skill and other characteristics that relate to that particular individual and in those particular circumstances. This point is easily understood by anyone who has worked very hard on an assignment or piece of work but has not been rewarded with the desired grade because their skill in writing up the results has not matched the effort involved.

Equity Theory

This theory is based on our view of how fairly we are treated when we compare ourselves with others. In its simplest form it follows the old maxim 'a fair day's pay for a fair day's work'. We are constantly putting a value on what we do, and grading the importance of the different factors making up our performance. The theory is reflected in equal pay legislation and equal opportunities. It is also seen when a group of workers feel their pay has fallen behind that of a comparable group. The media often expresses public concern when an industry chairperson is given a substantial pay increase but workers in the same industry are being made redundant or suffering wage cuts. It is also revealed in statements such as 'I spent hours on this; I expected a higher mark!'

Link: work of the personnel function

We expect our efforts to bring certain rewards. If the rewards do not meet our expectations we will probably change our behaviour or degree of effort accordingly. If people do not feel they are receiving a just reward, they may put in less effort, attempt to increase the reward or 'retire from the field' (be absent, leave the job and so on).

ACTIVITY 7.5

1. Find a newspaper story that demonstrates the above theory, that is, reports an incident in which an individual or a group of individuals are not receiving what appears to be just reward, either for their effort or in comparison with others in a similar position.

2. Identify, in the story you have selected:

    - The input of the individual or group.
    - The outcome or reward received.
    - Why the outcome was felt to be unfair.
    - The consequent effect on the individual or group.

3. Compare your findings with those of others in your group or class. Are there any common factors in the reasons why an outcome is felt to be unfair or in the effects of perceived inequity?

Goal Theory

As its name suggests, this is based on the setting of goals. From time to time we all set ourselves goals – whether to save up for a holiday, finish an assignment before our favourite TV programme starts, or become an accountant. In each of the above examples we have set a target. The target may be an encouragement to get a particular, perhaps unpleasant or difficult, task completed within a deadline, to fulfil a dream or to achieve something we want. Without a target or goal we tend to plod on aimlessly, never quite getting anywhere or achieving anything. The goal focuses the mind and the effort – it motivates.

Within the work environment, organisations too set goals. Goal theory maintains that, by making workers aware of the firm's goals, showing them their part in achieving those goals and setting targets together with each worker or group of workers, workers will be more motivated to achieve the organisation's objectives. If workers are personally involved in setting goals and can see or receive information of the effects of their part in the overall achievement, then their performance may well improve. We are all inclined to be more committed to decisions in which we have had a say than to those that are imposed upon us!

ACTIVITY 7.6   In Chapter 1 you listed five objectives that you wished to achieve within the next five years. Against each of those objectives, write down:

1.   What you need to do in order to fulfil the objective.
2.   The deadline for the achievement of the objective.
3.   How far you have progressed in working towards it.

7.3   THEORY Z

The origins of Theory Z, in Japan, result in a different approach to motivation in that it concentrates on the individual as part of the organisation rather than satisfaction of the individual's own needs.

Theory Z was developed by W. Ouchi, an American, in the 1980s from Japanese working and management styles. Not all Japanese working practices were easily transferable to Western industry but Ouchi felt that others could be successfully adapted.

In Theory Z the motivators include:

- Long-term employment.
- Identification with the organisation and its success.
- Shared decision making.
- Trust and respect between managers and workers.
- Loyalty and commitment to the organisation and fellow workers.

ACTIVITY 7.7   Compare Theory Z with the needs and process theories and identify major similarities and/or differences.

In this chapter, we have examined a number of theories on motivation, some based upon the definition of our actual needs, others relating to the process we adopt when trying to satisfy those needs. In the next chapter, we shall turn our attention to the approaches used by a variety of organisations to see how motivation works in practice, both for employer and employee.

SUMMARY

Motivation theories

Needs:

- Hierarchy of needs: Maslow
- ERG: Alderfer
- Two factor: Herzberg
- n-Ach: McClelland

Process:

- Expectancy: Vroom, Porter and Lawlor
- Equity
- Goal

Theory Z:

- Ouchi

8 MOTIVATORS AT WORK

8.1 MOTIVATION AND THE EMPLOYER

In Chapter 7 we looked at the theories of motivation – the needs theories, which examine the basis of motivation, and the process theories, which investigate circumstances affecting motivation.

But how do these theories relate to today's business organisations? Are they relevant? Do employers actually try to motivate their employees? If so, how do they go about it? To try to answer these questions we shall look at motivation in different work contexts and consider the techniques used by particular organisations.

It is important to remember that labour is a resource and like all resources used in business, it costs money. Consequently employers need to obtain maximum return on what they spend on resources. In terms of labour, what is the maximum return? Some factors are important to all jobs, others vary according to the nature of the work and the organisation. In the eyes of the employer, what are the characteristics of the 'perfect' employee? The following list makes some suggestions – you can probably add to it:

- Hard work
- Maximum effort
- High productivity
- Efficiency
- Increasing competence
- Quality of output

- Willingness to work
- Commitment and loyalty
- Enthusiasm and involvement
- Ability to learn and develop
- Contribute ideas
- Flexibility

But how does the employer set about obtaining and maintaining the best human resources? The personnel function of an organisation includes the practical aspects of recruitment and selection, training, pay and reward systems, and appraisal. In Part A we examined the role of managers. In our study of motivation we considered what is important to the individual – what the individual looks for at work, what makes him or her work harder. How do organisations put all these aspects together in order to get the best out of their human resources? We shall now look at a number of individual businesses to find out the techniques and approaches they use.

8.2 TRAINING

Training is generally recognised as an important factor in any successful organisation. An organisation must keep ahead in its particular industry. It must maintain high levels of quality and efficiency. It must remain competitive. In order to ensure that the workforce keeps up with the demands made on it, the training and retraining of staff will be necessary both to achieve these objectives and to keep abreast of the constant change that is a common factor in most business organisations today. At the same time training is important to the employee. It provides a greater opportunity for increased responsibility and the chance of promotion. It usually promotes confidence and pride in work, as well as increasing feelings of goodwill and commitment to the organisation.

Links: work of the personnel function; human resources

CASE 10
Campbell Grocery
Products Ltd

BACKGROUND

Campbell Grocery Products Ltd is a market leader in the manufacture and distribution of brand name and supermarkets' own label food products. Campbell's engineers service and carry out repairs on all the equipment and machinery used in the preparation and packaging of the food products. The engineers possess between them a variety of existing qualifications and/or experience.

The company, in setting up its training scheme for engineers, wanted to achieve the following objectives:

- The training should result in a qualification.
- It should be a nationally recognised qualification.
- All the engineers should have the same qualification regardless of the area in which they worked.
- The training should be skill based rather than knowledge based.
- It should take place in house, using the company's own machines.
- It should provide multiskilling.

The company decided that National Vocational Qualifications (NVQ) would provide the best route to meeting its objectives.

THE QUALIFICATION

NVQ qualifications cover a wide range of work areas. This enabled the company to set standard levels of performance throughout the company. Extra units could be undertaken in order to achieve multiskilling, and therefore greater flexibility within the workforce. NVQs are skill based qualifications and therefore demonstrate the ability to do the job. Where underpinning knowledge was still required, workers could be sent on courses provided locally. Otherwise, all training and assessment of competence could be carried out in-house and on the machines on which the engineers worked.

NVQs are a nationally recognised qualification which also enabled the company to recruit workers with the same qualifications and to know that the recruits' skills matched those of existing employees.

THE APPROACH

The plan was to divide the engineers into three groups, each starting the programme at six-monthly intervals.

For the scheme to work, managers involved had to be keen and enthusiastic. In house assessors were trained and their enthusiasm was important too. Managers needed to be available and willing to discuss the assessment plans with the groups and to deal with questions and problems.

Their view of the scheme would affect how the engineers viewed the scheme.

THE ENGINEERS

The engineers themselves became increasingly eager to join the scheme as the first group started the scheme and reported back. They liked the idea of being assessed on what they could do. They were particularly enthusiastic where competences related to their own specialist areas of work.

Turnover of staff in the engineering sections of Campbell's is low. As the engineers are on call to all departments of the factory, the work provides variety. There is limited alternative work for engineers in the immediate locality. Nevertheless, low turnover has one negative aspect – promotion opportunities are limited.

One further attraction of the scheme is its possible relevance to pay. The existing pay structure is qualification based rather than experience based. Gaining qualifications could increase pay, an attraction enhanced by the fact that this qualification is actually gained at work.

THE BENEFITS

For the company:

- The initial cost to the company (in spite of subsidies through the local TEC) is substantial but it is anticipated that future training costs will be reduced as a result of the programme and the recruitment of new workers who already have the same NVQ qualifications.
- Proves the competence of workers.
- Reveals any training needs.
- Ensures same level of competence if NVQ qualified workers are recruited.
- Gives uniformity of qualification.

- Less down-time needed for training.
- Multiskilled engineers.

For the engineers:

- A nationally recognised qualification which could be taken to another job.
- Possible increase in pay for achievement of the qualification.
- Opportunity to increase knowledge and range of skills.
- Although promotion prospects are limited, company is still providing opportunities for and encouraging development.

Pleased with the progress of the scheme, Campbell's is now considering the introduction of NVQ training in other areas of the organisation. The company is also running a Modern Apprenticeship programme where the apprentice gains NVQ Level 3 in Engineering Maintenance.

ACTIVITY 8.1
1. How may the introduction of the training programme have affected the way in which the engineers felt the company viewed them?
2. What factors affecting motivation and attitudes are revealed in this case study?
3. Explain if and how, in your opinion, the training would affect:

   - Quality of work.
   - Quantity of work.
   - Relationships (workers with each other, with their managers, with the company in general).

4. Which motivation theory do you think most closely applies to this case study, and why?

8.3   ORGANISATIONAL CULTURE AND CLIMATE

Culture and climate tend to be unique to an organisation. An organisation may have a reputation for a particular style – its culture: for example this organisation is considered to be benevolent in its approach to its employees; that organisation is known for its caring role in the community; another is seen as a market leader in its particular industry; one has a reputation for innovation; yet another is known for its policy towards the environment.

Link: corporate image

Within each organisation there also exists an atmosphere or climate arising from how the employees feel about the organisation. The organisation may be described by its staff as caring, or as a happy place in which to work. Alternatively it may be described in negative terms if relationships between different levels and groups are not good or if staff feel they are not treated fairly.

Lands' End is an American company that sells clothing by mail order. However Lands' End prefers the description 'direct merchants' to mail order and it describes its products as 'classic, timeless, and cut and sewn . . . clothing for leisure'. It also follows its founder's rather unusual instruction: 'Don't worry about what is best for the company. Worry about what is best for the customer'.

CASE 11
LANDS' END
DIRECT MERCHANTS
UK LTD

BACKGROUND

The title of the brochure which is given to all Lands' End's new employees reads:

'Welcome to Lands' End! We're happy you're joining us, and we're out to make you feel at home.'

The opening paragraph continues:

'Here is a warm handshake from the 7,900 member Lands' End family. The following pages are meant to provide you with some basic "getting acquainted" information. We hope it makes you feel more at home as a Lands' End employee.'

This is the fairly typical approach of a company where everyone dresses casually (jeans are much in evidence), no-one has special privileges (such as a company car) and ideas are positively encouraged.

Lands' End began in Chicago in 1963 with three employees. At first it dealt in equipment for the sailing enthusiast. Its first real clothing catalogue made its appearance in 1977. In 1992 it was included in the 100 Best Companies to work for in America. In 1993 it opened its UK operation. In 1994 it moved into Japan. It has now set up a distribution centre in Germany, operating from the UK division.

The rural town of Oakham, in Rutland, was chosen for the UK operation because it reflected the rural and community environment of the company's headquarters at Dodgeville, Wisconsin. The UK telephone and distribution centre started with 30 employees, it now has 300 staff.

CUSTOMER SERVICES AT OAKHAM

When staff are selected for the customer service department, skills and qualifications come second to the main question: 'Will this person fit in and be able to talk to our customers?'

Employment begins with two days of induction training. This concentrates on explaining the company's philosophy and its eight principles for doing business:

'Principle 1   We do everything we can to make our products better.

'Principle 2   We price our products fairly and honestly.
'Principle 3   We accept any return, for any reason, at any time.
'Principle 4   We ship [deliver] faster than anyone we know of.
'Principle 5   We believe that what is best for our customer is best for all of us.
'Principle 6   We don't buy branded merchandise with high protected markups . . . we have placed our contracts with manufacturers who have proven that they are cost-conscious and efficient.
'Principle 7   We operate efficiently. Our people are hard working, intelligent and share in the success of the company.
'Principle 8   We support no fancy emporiums [shops] with their high overhead.'

Customer sales staff work in teams of 12–18 members with a team leader. There is a base of permanent staff with 'regular' temporaries to help at peak order times. Customers order from a monthly catalogue which in addition to the detailed descriptions and photographs of the clothes, also includes information about the company, how the products are made and the materials used, and profiles of staff at Oakham.

Looking after the customer is the priority at Lands' End. Unlike many mail order operations, there is no recommended time limit to the length of the telephone call when the customer places an order. Staff are told to take as long as it needs to satisfy the customer – the call is freephone for the customer (prepaid envelopes are supplied for orders sent in by post).

THE COMPANY ENVIRONMENT

In 1984, the founder Gary Comer wrote to employees: 'The really important thing that makes Lands' End what it has become is people. You, me, everyone around us. It is what we do as people that makes this a great place to come to work.' The company continues to support that approach. The principle of 'taking ownership' is fostered, that is, to believe in what you are doing and in yourself. Employees are encouraged to feel involved and to participate. This includes putting forward ideas – and often in carrying them through too.

The pay scale is the same whether the employee packs goods, sews hems, takes orders or deals with customer queries. There are no company cars or reserved parking places for anyone. The benefits, which include pension schemes and staff discounts, are the same for all staff, at all levels.

Absenteeism is low. Careful selection is matched by exit interviews when employees leave – to find out whether anything can be improved upon.

ACTIVITY 8.2
1. Lands' End's primary objective is to serve and satisfy the customer. How do you think this influences its approach to employees?
2. What are Lands' End's objectives in relation to its employees?
3. What would you expect to be the result(s) of this approach?
4. Which motivation theories would you apply to this company and why?

ACTIVITY 8.3   Select an organisation that you feel you know quite well (for example where you work or have worked, where you spent your work experience, or even where you shop regularly).

1. Describe briefly what you see as the culture of the organisation (that is, its style and philosophy, the principles it sets).
2. Describe, from your experience, the climate of the organisation.
3. How do you think the culture and climate you have described affect the attitudes and motivation of the staff who work there?

8.4   IDENTITY AND SOCIAL RELATIONSHIPS

Link: product development and realisation

The theorists Maslow and Alderfer both recognised the need to belong, to be part of a group, and the need for social interaction. This is one of the motivating factors recognised and used by the following company. It is not an accident that the company's newspaper is called *Teamwork*!

CASE 12 TULIP INTERNATIONAL

BACKGROUND

The company name, Tulip International A/S, is probably less familiar to British consumers than its brand name DANEPAK. From its factories in Denmark, the UK and Germany, Tulip supplies bacon products world wide.

TULIP AT THETFORD

The Tulip factory at Thetford in Norfolk has 700 employees and on output of approximately 580 tons of bacon products each week. Until 1991, the factory was DANEPAK (the other parts of the company used different product names). Every effort had been made to create a Thetford factory identity to which employees could relate. Consequently, the sudden decision to change the Danish company name of Tulip and to use DANEPAK solely as a brand name caused an identity crisis for the workers at Thetford. The company newspaper is one of the ways in which the company is now trying to build up the broader identity of Tulip International. The newspaper sets out to link workers in the three countries and to keep them informed of what is happening in different parts of the company.

   Most of the employees at Thetford work on production lines. Each section covers a particular product range and consists of a number of production lines. Each line is made up of five to six separate jobs or tasks. In the sliced bacon section, for example, much of the work is routine and repetitive. Some of it is heavy. As most of it requires close attention to detail and concentration, it can also be stressful.

The working area is chilled. With the heat from machines and bodies, and the constant movement of swing doors into the area and between the pre-packaged and post-packaged parts of the line, it can also be extremely draughty. There is also a high noise level from the machines. Background music, popular with workers, has not been possible since the installation of new machines as this would take the noise above minimum health and safety levels. Management are currently trying to solve this particular problem.

Each worker on the line is trained to do all the jobs which make up the line. Jobs are rotated, usually at half-hour intervals, in order to provide some variety but also to reduce the risk of repetitive strain injury. In a seven-and-a half hour shift, the line closes down completely for two 15-minute breaks. The workers on the line take their breaks together in the staff canteen.

In order to further the 'identity' factor, each section at Thetford has selected its own colour code and the workers' hats (worn for hygiene reasons) are in the section colour. Each production line team stays together as a permanent work team, unless a move is specifically requested by one of the workers.

PAY AND PRODUCTIVITY

The Thetford factory is now moving towards a minimum wage policy for all workers as part of its strategy to maintain a happy workforce with low staff turnover. It is also aiming to bring the wages and conditions for agency workers (temporary staff taken on at peak times) nearer to those of full-time employees. The company also offers the opportunity to all workers to join its pension scheme.

Turnover of staff tends to be high in the first few months of employment but then drops dramatically. Absenteeism is not high for the type of work involved but efforts are being made to reduce it even further.

In spite of the international recession, in the last three years the Thetford factory has avoided redundancies. However, differences in currency levels in 1995 caused an unwelcome drop in profitability. As a result, a 5 per cent increase in productivity is now being sought.

Management has suggested that this increase could be achieved by ending the practice of closing down production lines for the fifteen-minute breaks. A staggered break time would allow the lines to keep producing. This would however prevent members of a work team taking their breaks together and bring to an end an important opportunity for social contact and group support.

Discussions are being held with the union to look for alternative ways of improving productivity. A change in some working practices has been suggested. For example, there is an unofficial 'toilet rota' – workers take it in turn to leave the line, ostensibly to 'go to the toilet'. There are also minutes lost at the start of the shift and after breaks, when work does not start immediately. These could provide opportunities for increasing productivity without losing the shared breaks.

ACTIVITY 8.4   1.   How was a sense of belonging encouraged at the Thetford factory? Suggest other methods the management could adopt.

2. Why would you expect pay and social interaction to be important to the production line workers at Thetford?

3. To what extent do you think Herzberg's theory can be applied to the production line workers at Thetford?

ACTIVITY 8.5 Carry out this activity in small groups, each group member taking on the role of one of the participants (for example the production manager, personnel officer, union representative, shop steward). Role-play the discussion between management and the union to try to reach agreement on how the increase in productivity should be achieved.

8.5 OWNERSHIP

Link: business organisations and systems

Employers frequently mention commitment and involvement when they are advertising for staff. Loyalty is also an important factor in a good employer–employee relationship. It is to be expected that those who both own and work in the business are most likely to show these qualities. However not all owners actually work in the business and few workers are also owners. The John Lewis Partnership, which consists of 22 department stores and over 100 Waitrose super-markets, is – in this respect at least – different from most other businesses.

CASE 13 JOHN LEWIS PARTNERSHIP THE PARTNERSHIP

'The concept of John Lewis as a Partnership extends to every single permanently employed member of our staff – everyone is literally a co-owner of the business. They have a say in the way the business is run through elected representation on various councils, and anyone can take a more active role by becoming representatives themselves. This direct involvement produces a special pride in work, which is reflected in the quality of our service to customers. Furthermore, being a Partner brings the tangible rewards of profit sharing. Every year, after all expenses have been met and money set aside for investment and development, the whole profit is shared out as a cash payment – the "Partnership Bonus".'

INCREASING PARTICIPATION

'The aim of the John Lewis Partnership . . . is not to be the biggest retail group in Britain but to be the best, the happiest and the most efficient. A great deal of energy is expended on examining the Partnership's social and political organisation to encourage the involvement of Partners in the running of their business, to add to the democratic elements in its systems and, as far as possible, to ensure its future by strengthening the institutions.'

THE PARTNERSHIP'S CHARACTER

'This constant development of the machinery of participation can be itemised and measured. What is less easy to assess is its effect upon the general atmosphere and character of the Partnership as experienced by those who work in it. Perhaps one indication is the extent to which some Partners are prepared to give their own time to organising leisure outings for their colleagues and the number of them who enjoy the company of fellow workers out of business hours. Another might be that the general trend of criticism and suggestions which come through the councils, committees for communication and letters to the journalism is a constructive one and serves to strengthen and expend the real practice of partnership.'

(Extracts from *John Lewis Partnership* and *John Lewis Partnership: Retail Management Training Scheme*, reproduced with the kind permission of the John Lewis Partnership).

ACTIVITY 8.6   In groups, discuss:

1.   The ways in which being a partner in the John Lewis Partnership would increase motivation and raise performance levels.
2.   The partnership principle, as operated by John Lewis, in relation to the process theories of motivation.

8.6   CAREER DEVELOPMENT

Link: self-development for career planning

Promotion opportunity is a strong motivator. In the current climate of improving efficiency and effectiveness in organisations, many companies are being streamlined by reducing the hierarchy and removing management tiers to create flatter organisational structures. Unfortunately this also limits promotion opportunities. Other organisations, ones that have grown rapidly, cannot offer the same opportunities once growth slows down or is curtailed. In these situations how does a company convince promising employees that their career prospects in the company are still good and discourage them from taking their skills elsewhere? Our next company profile looks at how Sun Microsystems has dealt with this particular problem.

CASE 14
SUN MICROSYSTEMS

Success brought a problem for Sun Microsystems, a market-leading manufacturer and supplier of network computer systems employing 13 000 people worldwide, including 1000 in the UK. The second computer company to achieve a billion-dollar turnover in a highly competitive market, it employs young, talented and ambitious people. To keep its market position the company has to ensure that it minimises staff turnover.

'About 70 per cent of our staff have one or two degrees, and these high flyers would have no problems in finding jobs elsewhere', says human resources director Paul Harrison. 'They were accustomed to the company's initial rapid expansion and exceptional job opportunities, but we are now containing our growth.'

A staff opinion poll revealed the perception that opportunities at Sun were shrinking. 'We needed to assure our employees that up is not the only way and that good career prospects still exist at Sun', says Harrison.

Together with organisational development consultants Blessing/White the company developed a tailored personal growth programme called Managing Your Career. All Sun's human resources team became certificated instructors and since 1992 have been running workshops for groups of employees which mix secretaries, engineers and managers from different departments.

'The process naturally interests people as it helps them focus on their skills and strengths', explains Paul Harrison.

There had been an assumption among staff that becoming a manager was the natural progression in a successful career, but the scheme demonstrated there were other options.

'As a result of Managing Your Career some employees are doing completely different jobs now', says Harrison. 'They are enjoying what they do and are therefore performing better.'

After five years in the marketing department of Sun Microsystems Zarina Khan had been promoted several times, and felt she had reached a plateau.

She took part in Sun's Managing Your Career programme and identified direct mail as an area she was interested in, which would also have business potential for the company. Together with her line manager she put together a new job specification. Two years on, Zarina Khan manages the direct mail and database sections at Sun.

Without the encouragement to take responsibility for her own career path, she says she would probably have left the firm.

(Reproduced with the kind permission of *Personnel Today* from *Personnel Today*, 28 March 1995. © *Personnel Today*).

ACTIVITY 8.7

1. Which aspects of the theories you have studied would apply to 'career development' as a motivator?
2. What do you think are the advantages both to the employer and to the employee of programmes such as Managing Your Career rather than the usual promotion opportunities?

8.7   SUMMARY

Motivation and the employer – motivational techniques:

● Training
● Organisational culture and climate
● Identity and social relationships
● Shared ownership
● Promotion and career development

PORTFOLIO ASSIGNMENT

This assignment is centred on the GNVQ Evidence Indicators. In it, you are required to:

● select an appropriate organisation to investigate;
● carry out a survey on the effects of motivation on performance in that organisation.

The Tasks

1. Carry out a survey in your selected organisation in order to obtain information on the following:

   ● What are people's attitudes to work?
   ● What affects their motivation?
   ● What motivators are used and are they appropriate and effective?

2. Write a report of your investigation. This should include:

   ● An explanation of how you carried out your survey.
   ● An analysis of the findings of your investigation.
   ● Reference to and application of relevant theories.
   ● The conclusions you have drawn from the results of your analysis, in particular the appropriateness and effectiveness of the motivators used by the employer.
   ● Recommendations you would make (on the basis of your survey) to increase motivation and change or improve the motivators used.

Guidelines to this assignment

When selecting the organisation in which to carry out your survey, it is useful to have some point of contact, such as:

- Your full-time employment.
- Your part-time employment.
- Work experience placement.
- Previous place of employment.
- A friend or relation who works there (can advise on suitability for your purpose, name of person to contact and so on).

When you have selected the organisation you must formally ask the appropriate person in the organisation for permission to carry out your survey.

You should aim to have a survey group of 20–30 individuals. These could be all the members (the *population*) of the organisation (if no more than 30) or all the members of one department of the organisation (if no more than 30). If the organisation or department is too large for you to survey the population, you will need to conduct your survey with a *sample*. In this case you must ensure that your sample is representative of the population. This will depend upon the population in question but you need to take into consideration, for example, age, gender, job or status in order to obtain a fair sample.

You may wish to refer back to the introductory assignment in Chapter 1 for guidelines on constructing questionnaires and writing reports.

Core skills: communication; application of number; information technology

PART C EXAMINING THE BEHAVIOUR OF GROUPS IN THE WORKPLACE

⑨ THE NATURE OF GROUPS

9.1 THE ASSIGNMENT

Links: teamworking; people in business organisations (intermediate)
Core skill: working with others

It is intended that the portfolio assignment for Part C (located at the end of Chapter 12) should be undertaken alongside the reading and study as it is important that you use what you are learning from your own group to help you to understand the theory. Ideally the assignment should take a number of weeks to complete, but it could be undertaken as part of the activities being carried out for another unit that includes group work. Alternative activities (Method A or Method B) are suggested in the assignment in order to meet the different needs of different students (for example full-time or part-time). Method A is designed to be carried out in student groups and may therefore be more appropriate to full-time students. Method B needs to be carried out in the workplace and is therefore suitable for students on part-time courses and those for whom a student group is not practicable, or for students who have part-time jobs or are undertaking the assignment while on work experience.

Many of the activities in Part C provide an opportunity to put together and prepare material that can be used in the portfolio assignment.

You should also note that working in a group produces its own problems. There will be disagreements and arguments; you will no doubt find it difficult to get on with some members of your group; and some members of your group will almost certainly not behave or carry out their work as you would wish. Do not worry about this – *it is part of the experience of this assignment* and is very important to your understanding of how groups behave. You will not benefit from the assignment if you work with your closest friends. It is therefore suggested that the group members are selected by your tutor or by 'drawing names from a hat'. This does not apply, of course, if you are carrying out the assignment in the workplace, where you will have little say in the membership of your work group.

9.2 WHAT IS A GROUP?

A group is a number of people who come together to share a common goal or purpose. A group has three important characteristics: its members interact with each other – they communicate and depend upon each other in some way; its members are conscious of each other, recognising that each person has a part or role to play in the group; and the members actually see themselves as a group, a body of people with a shared objective.

The following example demonstrates the difference between a collection of individuals and a group, and to show the point at which and the reason why individuals become a group.

CASE 15 **THE TRAIN JOURNEY**	The train from York to Leeds was running on time when as it began to pull out of the last stop before its arrival at Leeds. In the second compartment it was relatively quiet. At each station along the route, one or two passengers had alighted from or boarded the train. Most passengers appeared to be travelling silently alone, although there was a low hum of conversation among those travelling together. Suddenly the train came to a halt, still in the station. At first no-one showed any concern. After several minutes, however, it began to occur to people that something was amiss and anxiety showed on some faces. Then an announcement was made by the train conductor to the effect that, due to an obstruction on the line ahead, there would be some delay. For a moment there was silence, then someone made a joke about British Rail and everyone laughed. Passengers started to talk to each other – 'Oh dear, I have an appointment', 'I have another train to catch, I shall miss the connection', and so on. There was a buzz of conversation as people discussed the delay and the difficulties it would cause them. As time went on the conversations became more general as people began talk about other topics. Some time later the passengers were told that a coach was waiting outside to take them the rest of the way to Leeds, and that they should leave the train, go over the bridge and make their way to the exit where the coach was waiting. The passengers began to gather together their possessions. One passenger helped a mother with a small child by carrying the pushchair. Others carried the cases of an elderly couple and assisted them over the bridge. People continued to chat and to help each other in the transfer to the coach. Once on the coach, conversation gradually declined. At Leeds the passengers went their separate ways.

At the start of this incident the passengers were simply a collection of individuals travelling on the same train. There was no interaction between them. In most cases each person probably scarcely noticed the others and would have found it difficult to describe them later.

When the train was held up they suddenly shared a common problem. All had the same objective – to get to their destination – and were sharing the same experience. For that period they became a group. As a group, the members interacted, talking to each other. They had a common goal and began to show some concern and support for each other. Once the crisis was over and they were on their way again, they gradually separated into unconnected individuals as their common ground disappeared. The group identity only lasted until the problem had been resolved.

ACTIVITY 9.1   Describe a situation similar to the one outlined above where you have temporarily become part of a group with which you have had no contact before or since (for example on holiday, on a short training course, as a hospital patient, stuck in a lift).

9.3 GROUPS AT WORK

In Chapter 2 we looked at the Hawthorne Studies. One of the experiments carried out by Elton Mayo and the Harvard researchers was that of the relay assembly test room. There the researchers studied a group of employees set up by management to work under a variety of conditions to monitor the effects of the different conditions imposed. During the experiment the researchers noticed how the workers developed into a closely knit social group. In the bank wiring observation room experiment the large number of workers were observed to divide themselves into smaller social groups and the researchers noted the effects this had on the workers and their productivity. The groups would set the level of work they were going to maintain, and even when offered a pay incentive they did not increase their level of productivity. As a result of the Hawthorne Studies, more attention was given to the social aspects of work in meeting employee needs and to the ways in which groups affected, and could benefit, the work environment.

Types of Group

In organisations, there are essentially two types of group: formal and informal.

Formal Groups

Formal groups are 'official' groups, those set up by management as part of the structure of the organisation. Most of these groups appear on the organisation chart of the business.

Formal groups usually have a specific area of work, for example in an accounts office, a sales team, the production area. Some formal groups are set up to carry out a specific task, for example a group consisting of people selected from different departments of the business to plan and surprise the move to new premises. Once the move has been completed, this group's purpose has been fulfilled and it is disbanded, the members returning to their former work and groups. Similar short-term project groups operate only for the duration of the particular task they are set up to carry out, but those that appear in the organisational chart exist in the long term and are not limited to one particular task, although they do have a particular area of work. Their membership may also be stable, so individuals work in the same group with the same people for a number of years.

Informal Groups

Informal groups are 'unofficial' groups and are not set up by the organisation. These groups are based on personal and social relationships within the organisation. They are not bound by the organisational structure so you may find a social group within one section or spread across several departments or levels of the hierarchy. These groups may arise simply from people working together and therefore may be all or part of a formal group. Groups also arise from friendships that develop between people working in different parts of the organisation, or because of common interests (for example all play for the local football team). Sometimes relationships and links are developed deliberately for convenience or self-interest, for example to ensure that your photocopying is done quickly (regardless of a 'queue'), or that your post goes out that night even though the mailroom's deadline has been missed, or perhaps to ensure that your customers' orders are always dealt with promptly.

Networks can develop across the organisation that are completely separate from the formal structure but provide additional channels of communication and information flow.

It is quite possible that in some networks, like the one in Figure 9.1, some members do not know each other, but nevertheless the link is maintained through the interconnected relationships.

Informal groups also have leaders but here the leader is selected by the members of the group (consciously or without realising it). A formal group rarely has any choice in the selection of the manager or

Figure 9.1 A network

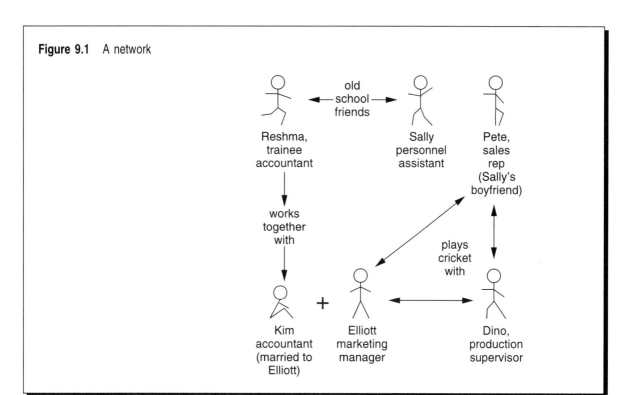

supervisor, but often an informal leader may emerge who is not the manager and problems can arise if the objectives of the leader differ from those of the manager. Sometimes the leader of the informal group changes according to the circumstances facing the group. Some groups are unaware of who is the leader or even that there is a leader. Often students, when working together on a task, will maintain that they share the roles equally and no-one has emerged as leader. However an outside observer may notice that one student adopts a stronger role at the planning stage, another coordinates the collection of information, while a third takes charge when the report is put together – leadership is there throughout but it changes when different qualities are required.

9.4 WHEN IS A GROUP A TEAM?

Links: teamworking; roles and responsibilities of supervisors

A team may be described as a particularly well-developed and coordinated group. Within a team the bonding and interdependence have become very strong. Some organisations send groups of workers on special teambuilding courses in order to create this level of cohesiveness or bonding. The objective of such courses is to put people into a situation where they are dependent upon each other for the completion of the task. On some Outward Bound types of course, they may actually be dependent upon each other for their physical safety and survival. These courses aim to give team members a greater understanding of their own and others' strengths and weaknesses and to develop their ability to work together. It is expected that they will then be able to apply these skills in the work situation.

An effective team is very closely knit, supportive of each other, able to communicate well with each other and appreciative of the value of each member's contribution.

CASE 16
CARNAUDMETALBOX

(NB: items marked * are explained at end.)

CARNAUDMETALBOX manufactures cans for the food industry thoughout the world. By the end of the 1980s, the hierarchy of the Wisbech factory of CARNAUDMETALBOX had become complex and cumbersome. The old style of management had encouraged competition between work crews as a means of increasing production. This was no longer successful. As a result of that strategy, there was little communication and absolutely no cooperation between shifts or even between crews on the same shift. The system was inefficient. An increasingly skilled workforce was ready for more responsibility, which the system did not permit.

A change of manager at the factory was the starting point for a programme of change. This led in 1991 to the decision to follow a Total Quality route. The first stage in this process was to encourage more team working. A group of supervisors developed teambuilding activities to take place at the nearby Mepal Water Sports Centre. Gradually every member of the workforce took part in exercises such as raftbuilding in order to develop the required team skills.

Unfortunately, just as enthusiasm was growing, the programme had to slow down during lengthy pay discussions between management and union. To keep up some momentum, team based exercises were introduced into the factory environment to look at ways of improving the operational process. Overmanning provided the opportunity for workers to be taken from the production line in order to participate in activities involving brainstorming*, the Pareto principle*, force field analysis* statistical process control*, and so on while developing team skills.

In 1992, the Customer–Supplier Partnership exercise took the programme back on course. Workers examined the relationship between the company and its customers and suppliers and, at the same, began to experience how it would feel if the full team approach was adopted. Visiting members of the company's senior management from both the UK and abroad were invited to take part in the role play exercises with the workers. Learning took place on all sides – managers became workers, workers played the part of customers or suppliers. The next decision was to move the Wisbech factory towards working in autonomous teams*.

On 5 January 1993 a business decision was taken to create centres of excellence, focussing factories on selected can-making processes in order to achieve the highest quality level. The result of this decision was that both cans and ends would no longer be made at the Wisbech factory, only the cylinder or can body. The can ends would be made at another factory. As a result, the press department in Wisbech would be closed and 131 workers from the press and other departments would be made redundant. In the event, there were only seven compulsory redundancies, all the others were achieved voluntarily.

Nevertheless, in spite of this, the planned programme continued and on 1 May 1993 the Wisbech factory was encouraged to operate autonomous teams with immediate effect. The management and supervisory hierarchy was abolished. In future a small management team would head the factory and, with six process managers (two for each of the three shifts), that comprised the total management structure. The workforce operated in seven manufacturing teams. Support functions, such as engineers, were reduced by 75 per cent and the functions contracted out to preferred suppliers.

In November 1993, the reorganisation was reviewed. The process managers were replaced by team managers. Each team manager was responsible for a production line (or lines in some cases) over a full 24-hour period rather than by shift. Since the team manager would, obviously, only be there for eight or nine of the 24 hours, the operators working on that line in each shift did so without supervision. The team approach meant that supervision was no longer needed. The team dealt with its own problems. For example, if repairs were needed, the team called out the contractor and explained the problem. If a customer had a complaint, the team and the customer got together and sorted it out. Just in case of a major emergency, a 'responsible person' was always on site but otherwise everything was handled by the team. Hence the name 'autonomous teams'.

In 1995, an attitude survey was carried out. Of the 250 employees surveyed, 201 replied. Of these, 50–60 per cent expressed enthusiasm for the new work system. Of the remainder, only 15 per cent were unhappy with the system.

Although there had been an initial cost in terms of new machines, the factory identified the following results:

- cost per can per employee was drastically reduced
- the same number of cans was produced, in spite of the reduction in the workforce
- levels of supervision were completely removed
- direct contact between a team and a supplier or a customer saved time and simplified communication (it no longer passed through several layers of management)
- workers responded to the increased responsibility and control they had over their work.

A Customer/Supplier Partnership Team looks at any problems arising from those relationships and suggests possible improvements.

A second attitude survey will be carried out at Wisbech during 1996. Then it might be time to consider whether or not the teams should be responsible for their own hiring and firing!

* Key to terms

Autonomous teams: production method and workgroup structure designed to work together; group accepts more responsibility for carrying out the tasks and meeting standards and targets.

Brainstorming: a technique used to generate as many ideas as possible; members of group put forward ideas quickly and without comment, criticism or discussion.

Force field analysis: a way at looking at problems that have factors holding them back as well as pushing them forward.

Pareto principle: otherwise known as the 80/20 principle; for example 80 per cent of the business comes from 20 per cent of the customers, 80 per cent of staff complaints comes from 20 per cent of the staff.

Statistical process control: a system of checking a proportion of items going through production against set standards.

ACTIVITY 9.2
1. Describe the style of management at CarnaudMetalbox prior to 1991.
2. What sort of techniques were used for teambuilding at the company?
3. What were the benefits of the autonomous teams approach to:
   - The company?
   - The workers?

9.5 FACTORS THAT AFFECT GROUPS

Link: individuals and organisation (intermediate)

In the work environment there are a number of factors that may affect the way a group behaves. These range from the actual size of the group to the environment in which the organisation operates. Each may influence the group to a greater or lesser extent, so it is important to be aware of them.

The Nature of the Task

This is probably the most obvious factor to affect the group. For example the members of a hospital surgical team carrying out an operation have very individual and precise roles and need to coordinate and anticipate each other's actions and requirements. A workgroup in a supermarket may all work on the checkout, fill shelves, deal with customer enquiries, check incoming goods, order new stock and so on, and change and interchange their jobs according to what is needed at the time.

A group may be affected by the equipment and machinery used. The layout of the machinery or noise level may limit social interaction while working. Some types of work allow conversation to flourish without affecting the flow of operation or productivity – in many routine and boring jobs this can be very important.

Increasingly, in many types of work social interaction as well as business may be via computer. Members of a group whose contact with each other is by this method will set up patterns of behaviour that differ from those of a group working together in one room.

The Environment in which the Group Works and in which the Organisation Operates

The immediate surroundings and work situation have an effect on a group just as they affect the individual. Carry out the activity below to consider this further.

ACTIVITY 9.3   In what ways do you think the following environments and/or type of work would affect that particular work group:

1. Coalminers working underground (for example the possible dangers, being detached or far away from rest of the world when underground).
2. Sales office team dealing with telephone orders.
3. Staff in a busy restaurant.
4. Teachers in a school or college.
5. Machinists sewing garments in a clothing factory.

The culture and climate of the organisation itself have an influence on the groups working in that organisation. In a company that has a reputation for looking after the well-being of its workers you would expect a similar concern to be shown by the workers for each other. In an organisation that has a more authoritarian approach, that approach may be reflected in its workgroups. In a company that operates in a very competitive industry (such as computer software) you may find more intense rivalry between workgroups and between individuals within groups as the need to compete in order to succeed or survive will exist at all levels.

The Group Itself

The composition of the group is a fundamental factor in how it behaves. You have no doubt been part of a group when someone left or a new person joined, and said to yourself: 'It doesn't seem the same any more'. Any change in the membership of a group will affect the group in some way. When a new person is appointed to a workteam it takes some time for the team to adjust to that person and to achieve its optimum effectiveness again. Everyone in the team has to adjust – you cannot fit the new member exactly into the 'gap' that someone else has left.

Group size is also relevant to the behaviour of a group. If a group becomes too large within its context, it will split into subgroups or factions. The appropriate size will depend upon the situation but most groups tend to divide if there are more than ten members.

A group is also influenced by its status within the organisation and its importance in relation to the organisation as a whole. If it is a long-standing or well-established group it will behave differently from a group whose membership is constantly changing or a group with a limited lifespan, an *ad hoc* group.

Most groups are strongly influenced by their manager or leader and by his or her style of leadership. The opportunities for social interaction vary according to a group's circumstances – these are likely to be greater in an informal group than in a formal one, and will be even less in a formal group whose members are separated by machinery or equipment.

9.10 SUMMARY

A group:

- A number of people who knowingly come together – common goal or purpose

Groups at work:

- Hawthorne Studies
- Types of group: formal, informal

Teams:

- Autonomous teams

Factors affecting groups:

- Nature of task
- Environment
- Group itself

10 ROLES IN GROUPS

10.1 GROUP ROLES

Within groups individuals take on roles, that is, each person plays a particular part in the group. For example in a football team the players occupy certain positions on the field – backs defend the goal area and prevent the other side from scoring, forwards aim to get past the other team's defence and score goals. Within a team more precise roles may be worked out, for instance one player sets up a situation to enable another to kick the ball into the goal. For a particular game, defence strategies may be created to deal with the opposing team's method of attack.

Similarly, if we look at the organisation chart of a business we can recognise certain functional roles. An accountant can be expected to work on financial aspects of the business. A production supervisor is obviously involved in the manufacture of the product, but the title also indicates a particular place in the hierarchy with responsibility for other workers. The range of duties and responsibilities attaching to the role is usually defined in a job description. Roles are part of the formal structure of the organisation and also define the hierarchy and relative status within the organisation as a whole and within a particular work section.

Even within informal groups a structure develops. People take on roles and play a particular part within the group. Think of your circle of friends. Is there one person who always tries to cheer up everyone else – 'is good for a laugh'? Is there another to whom everyone turns when they have a problem or need a 'shoulder to cry on'? Is it always the same person who says, 'Come on, we'd better get some work done now!'? Perhaps there is one person who always seems to be in charge, to whom everyone else refers for final decisions or approval.

An individual may belong to a number of different groups within the organisation. For example a particular individual may be a member of a workgroup, the health and safety committee, and the social club committee. In each group the individual's role will probably be different. In the workgroup, assuming the individual is a supervisor, she or he will be in charge of the team; as a supervisor, she or he will be part of a peer group of supervisors; on the health and safety committee, she or he may be the union representative; and she or he could be chair of the social club committee.

ACTIVITY 10.1   The staff social club committee of BJK Ltd is elected at the annual general meeting of the social club. The club runs social and sports activities for all employees (including former employees who have retired). At present the club is short of funds, and the committee's first priority is to look at activities that will bring in more income. The committee is meeting for the first time since this year's election. The members are:

- Dan (production supervisor)
- Leon (personnel assistant)
- Ellie (accountant)
- Mario (sales representative)
- Renata (marketing manager)
- Chris (computer technician)
- Jon (production operator)

The main agenda items for the first meeting are:

- The election of officers (chair, secretary and treasurer).
- Subscription rates (previously £5.00 per annum).
- Club's cash crisis: raising funds.

In groups of seven, role play the characters named above and conduct the new committee's first meeting. You should aim to give the person you are playing a 'character' (do not play it as yourself), so it would be useful to allow a few minutes before the committee starts its meeting for each person to think him or herself into the character. At the end of the session, discuss:

1.   How you developed the role you were given, such as what particular characteristics and qualities you assigned to the character.
2.   How you viewed the personalities developed by the other members of your group.
3.   How the group developed – did any hierarchy or structure become apparent, did the person elected as chair conduct the meeting, or did someone else 'manage' everyone, and so on?

10.2 TYPICAL ROLES

R. M. Belbin undertook research into the composition of groups and later described the roles that turned up in management teams. Belbin defined the eight most useful team roles as follows:

Belbin's types	Likely characteristics
Company worker	Works hard, does as told, sensible
Chairman	Keeps calm, confident, does not lose cool, able to draw others together and keep to objectives
Shaper	Pushes ahead, will challenge what is said. outspoken, temperamental perhaps, often impatient with others
Plant	Very individual, imaginative and knowledgeable, serious about task, not always practical
Resource investigator	Outgoing, enthusiastic, capable of contacting and communicating with people, curious, likes challenge and new ideas but may lose interest after a while
Monitor–evaluator	Tends to be serious, does not flap, good judgement, level headed, not inspiring or able to motivate others
Team worker	Sociable, can work well with others and is sensitive to them, promotes team spirit
Completer–finisher	Conscientious, careful and orderly person, wants to get things 'just right', able to see things through to the end but tends to worry.

Roles may change or individuals may take on different roles at different times so that there is flexibility within the group to meet changing circumstances. Belbin also suggested that teams should be mixed in order to obtain a balance of team whose members worked well together. Teams tend not to work well if:

- All the members are clever.
- None of the members are clever.
- All the members have similar personalities.
- There are strong personality clashes.
- Some members are not able to fulfil their role in the team.
  (This may happen if one member is often absent or does not carry out the tasks assigned to him/her.)

There are other ways of describing the types that commonly occur in groups. You may recognise some of the following and can probably add more to the list:

- *Innovator*: has lots of good ideas.
- *Peacekeeper*: good at patching up disagreements and calming things down.
- *Leader*: draws group together, consolidates work and effort, sets the direction, members refer/defer to him/her.

- *Joker*:   relaxes group, tries to stop things getting too serious, likes making people laugh.
- *Organiser*:   likes structured approach, keen to plan and get things done, methodical, good at assigning tasks and monitoring them.
- *Follower*:   always supports leader, loyal.
- *Dominator*:   always wants own way, bossy.
- *Investigator*:   good at (and likes) finding things out, willing to ask for information and talk to people.

If you can identify some of these or some of Belbin's types, then you have a typical workgroup that is probably experiencing the difficulties of working together.

ACTIVITY 10.2   At this point you should compare your assignment group with Belbin's types and the other roles listed above to see if you can identify any of them in your group.

Using Belbin's criteria, do you think that your group has a balanced mix of individuals? (You may wish to carry out this comparison with the 'committee' group used in Activity 10.1 instead of your assignment group.)

Most of the role types described can be placed in one of two categories: those whose role is directed towards getting the task done (*task roles*) and those whose role is directed towards supporting and encouraging the group (*maintenance roles*). Both categories are important in achieving successful group work. It is useful to remember this when looking at the individual contributions of the members of the group. One or two individuals may not appear to have carried out as much of the task as others but may have been vital in keeping the group together and working in harmony or in cheering them up when spirits were low.

ACTIVITY 10.3   Using your answers to Activity 10.1, identify which roles in your group are task roles and which are maintenance roles.

Occasionally a group will find it has one member who for some reason never fully becomes part of the group (an outsider) or at some point actively withdraws from the group and the work. Sometimes a group will always blame one person for things that go wrong and may push him or her to the fringes of the group, or even exclude that person from the group – this is called *scapegoating*.

10.3 ROLE PROBLEMS

Typecasting

Within a group, a member may assume or take on a particular role or the group may assign that role to her or him. Sometimes individuals find they cannot escape the role – rather like an actor or actress who plays a role in a TV series and finds that he or she is always identified with that role, even years after the series has finished. This can prove limiting or frustrating for the individual who wishes to change or have other qualities recognised.

Role Ambiguity

An individual who is not quite sure what the assigned role involves may become unhappy and upset because there is confusion about what is expected of him or her. This is described as *role ambiguity* and it may also occur if the individual sees the role differently from the way it is seen by the other members of the group. Role ambiguity often occurs when someone is new to a role. The defined role (such as in a job description) may not give a clear indication of the duties and responsibilities attached to it. The new holder of the post may pick up conflicting information on the role from those around, such as what her or his predecessor did or what they think ought to be done. There is also a period when the new person is settling into the group. There is sometimes an expectation that a new employee will fit exactly into the place of the former holder of the post. In fact there is likely to be a period of adjustment for *all* the members of the workgroup to accommodate the new member as no one can – nor should try to – fill the role exactly as it was before as she or he will bring new personal qualities and skills to the job and the group.

Role Conflict

Individuals frequently suffer from *role conflict* – they have more than one role to fulfil. Role conflict can arise in situations such as the following:

- *Conflicting roles within the same job*: a manager is responsible for disciplining one of his staff who is frequently late for work, but the manager is also responsible for the welfare of his staff and knows that the member of staff is late because of a sick spouse.

- *Conflict between two separate roles at work*: as a worker and as a trade union representative or perhaps a health and safety representative.
- *Conflict between a role at work and a role outside work*: the role of manager, which demands that long hours are worked, and the role of a parent who wants to spend time with a child or children.

Role Overload and Role Underload

A person can suffer from role overload or role underload. In *role overload* the individual has more roles, probably of a widely varying nature, than she or he can handle. This leads to stress. In the opposite situation, *role underload*, the person expects to take on – and believes she or he is capable of taking on – more roles or responsibilities than she or he is given. This leads her or him to feel undervalued, which may create a different type of stress.

Role Stress

Stress has been identified as a major problem in the modern workplace. What do we mean by stress? Imagine you have just bought a poster. You ask for it to be rolled so that it will not crease. The shop assistant places a rubber band around the roll. If the rubber band is too loose, there is no tension in it and it will not hold the roll firmly together. But if the rubber band is stretched too tightly it will crease the paper and may even break. Stress is very much like an elastic band. Insufficient tension or absence of stress will leave us lacking stimulation, lethargic, bored, and eventually perhaps depressed. Too much stress and we become tense and anxious, and we may feel we cannot cope and become depressed, leading even to physical illness. Role stress is one form of stress that can be suffered at work and it affects the effectiveness of both the individual and the group.

In the group situation, any of the above role problems will prevent the group from working effectively and may lead to relationship problems. For example one member may feel that she or he has too many different roles to fulfil whereas another feels that she or he is not being allowed to take on the responsibilities of which she or he is capable.

ACTIVITY 10.4   Describe any situations in which you are involved that are causing or might cause you any of the role problems outlined above.

ACTIVITY 10.5   *Either*

1. Discuss role problems with your assignment group and try to identify any difficulties of this sort that are being or may be experienced by members of the group. Consider how you might resolve any such difficulties.

Or

2. Consider the group at work upon which you have based your assignment. From discussions with your colleagues in the group, can you identify any role difficulties being experienced? How could you resolve them?

10.4   SUMMARY

The nature of roles:

- In the organisational structure
- In groups

Types of roles:

- Belbin's roles in management teams
- Balanced teams
- Task roles and maintenance roles

Role problems:

- Typecasting
- Ambiguity
- Conflict
- Overload and underload
- Stress

11 GROUP BEHAVIOUR

11.1 HOW GROUPS DEVELOP

Link: teamworking

In 1965 B. W. Tuckman developed a model of group development. If you have kept a diary or log of your assignment group, as suggested, you could check this against Tuckman's stages of development to see if there are similarities in the way in which your group has developed. If you are carrying out the assignment at work you will probably need to select a different group with which to test out Tuckman's ideas – a group that has recently been set up for a short period in order to carry out a particular task rather than a long-term workgroup.

Tuckman wrote that groups move through four stages in the process of their development:

Stage 1: Forming

This is initial stage when the members first come together. The members are getting to know each other, working out their roles in the group, establishing a leader, gathering information about the task and how to proceed with it.

Stage 2: Storming

This is a period of disagreement and conflict. Different views are put forward on how the task should be carried out. Members may be jockeying for position within the group. Relationships are being worked out – not always smoothly. Members struggle to learn how to work together and to establish methods of working.

Stage 3: Norming

At this point the group has 'got its act together'. Members have reached an acceptable way of working together, relationships are smoother (members may still not agree but have found ways of accepting or tolerating each others' views). The group is beginning to develop a group identity, to think of itself as a group. Patterns of behaviour are developing. Group standards and rules of operation are being set up – norms. The group is now able to start tackling the task.

Stage 4: Performing

The group is now operating as a team and begins to carry out the task(s).

ACTIVITY 11.1   Identify and describe these stages of development in *one* of the following:

1.   Your assignment group.
2.   Any other short-term group of which you are a member.

11.2   ASPECTS OF GROUP BEHAVIOUR

There are some types of behaviour that are characteristic of groups. You will be able to check whether these characteristics appear in the assignment group in which you are working or in any other groups with which you are involved or have the opportunity to observe.

Size and Structure

Group size affects the way in which a group behaves. As we saw in the Hawthorne Studies, the large group of workers in the bank wiring observation room experiment subdivided into smaller groups. This is a characteristic of large groups. The larger the group, the less some members feel able to join in but the greater the range of ideas and skills available to the group.

A group will also be affected by its structure, which often depends upon the relationships within the group and the way in which members communicate with each other. In may also depend upon the nature of the task on which the group is working. A group working side by side in a line may only be able to communicate along the line. In a formal workgroup all communication may go through the manager or supervisor at the top of the hierarchy. In other groups word passes from person to person in a circle. In one type of group structure all communication is via one person in the centre (this could happen where sales representatives make contact through the central sales office). In many groups, of course, everyone communicates with everyone else without a clearly defined pattern, but if the group has a strong and vocal leader, more communication may go to and from the leader than between the other members.

Norms and Conformity

As a group develops it begins to establish its own rules and standards of behaviour, usually called *norms*. These develop gradually and the group may have been unaware of the process. For example is it the norm in your circle of friends to work hard or to 'loaf around' quite a lot? If you belong to the latter type of group, how easy would it be for one person to decide that she or he now wishes to work hard? What would the other group members say or do?

Most of us are familiar with that well-known norm: 'you don't tell on your friends'. In some groups one of the norms may relate to the way members dress. In another, use of jargon or coded language will identify the members. A certain pattern of behaviour may become established, such as: 'we always go to the pub after the match'.

ACTIVITY 11.2
1.   Choose a group of which you are a member and describe any rules or patterns of behaviour established by that group.
2.   Suggest groups that may be identified by each of the following:

   - Dress
   - Jargon/'special' language
   - Beliefs
   - Attitudes.

In some workgroups norms are set up about the level of productivity (this happened in the Hawthorne Studies bank wiring observation room experiment). A group will reach an acceptable (to the group) level and speed of working – a newcomer who works faster may be very quickly brought into line, perhaps initially by joking then by ruder comments if she or he does not readily conform! There may be norms about which company rules you break and which you don't, how you treat the boss, or where you all go for lunch.

However norms can also create problems, for example when management needs to increase productivity so that the firm can compete in its product market or survive in a difficult economic climate.

ACTIVITY 11.3   In Case 12 (Tulip International A/S – Chapter 8) what norms were set up by the workers that, it was suggested, could be given up in order to increase productivity?

Norms are important to groups because they help foster group identity, bind the group members together and encourage *conformity*. Most people are conformists – we don't like to be too different or too conspicuous. We don't want to stand out, we 'go along with the crowd'. People who do not conform are often seen as eccentric, odd or troublemakers. There are some people, such as film stars, artists and so on, that we expect not to conform and are quite disappointed if they appear as ordinary as ourselves!

Conformity is part of what is referred to as group *cohesiveness*. This is the result of the process of building up loyalty and commitment to the group, of sharing in its identity and of feeling that you belong. When we talk of teambuilding exercises we are actually referring to activities designed to build up that cohesiveness.

Groupthink

Sometimes a group may reach the point where its members over-conform. The group sees itself as always right and invincible, and the outside world as wrong. It fails to recognise its weaknesses and the signs of its own problems. Dissension or disagreement by a member is not permitted and members become afraid to voice their opinions. This is known as *groupthink* and can be dangerous.

Group Polarisation

Groups show a tendency to be more cautious in their decisions than an individual acting alone would be. But sometimes a group may take a decision that is more risky than any one individual member would have taken alone. When groups take extreme positions it is referred to as *group polarisation*. This often happens when a group is under pressure from outside and therefore believes it must support its decisions more strongly. In such circumstances, as in groupthink, it is important that all opinions are heard.

ACTIVITY 11.4
1. Discuss the problems that may arise for an individual from being 'different'?
2. Discuss when might it be important for an individual not to conform.
3. Identify situations (in history, current world affairs or your own experience) in which you think there is evidence of 'groupthink'.

Conflict

If you have been carrying out the assignment for Part C you have probably already experienced conflict within the group. Conflict is an inevitable part of group behaviour, inevitable because a group is made up of individuals, each with his or her own ideas so there are bound to be differences of opinion and view. However conflict does not have to be a bad thing. Some conflict is constructive and will in fact help the group to work more effectively by producing a variety of ideas and opinions, by ensuring that the group explores different approaches, and by clarifying roles and positions within the group. Sometimes it is better to have opportunities for people to air their grievances and get them 'off their chests' as this enables problems to be resolved and the group to move forward.

Differences that are buried or left to simmer frequently prove more destructive in the long run. If conflict is not handled in a positive and useful way the group may become sidetracked. The conflict becomes more important than the task – it may even replace the task in the group's objectives. Such conflict may ultimately break up the group.

It is therefore important that a group learns to manage its conflict and for individuals to adopt behaviour that enables them to communicate and resolve their areas of conflict. Techniques for reducing unnecessary conflict in a group include shared goals, improving communication within the group and exchanging ideas, avoiding competition between members and improving group and teamwork skills. Like CARNAUDMETALBOX in Case 16 and Nuclear Electric in Case 5, many organisations now introduce teambuilding into their training programmes in order to improve these skills.

ACTIVITY 11.5
NB: You may wish to use your assignment group as the basis for this activity.

1. Describe the nature of a particular conflict in a group of which you are a member?

2.   What was the effect of the conflict on the group?
3.   How did the group deal with the conflict?

Conflict not only occurs within a group, it also occurs between groups. Tribal warfare, fights between supporters of rival football teams and industrial strikes are all examples of conflict between groups. Within organisations conflict may arise between different departments or sections of departments. The mere process of group development divides the group members from those not in the group. What sometimes starts off as friendly rivalry or competition between groups may develop to the point where it prevents the groups from working together. The people in sales may think that the production department is being uncooperative in meeting order dates. Those in the production department do not like what they see as the personnel department's interference in health and safety procedures in the factory. The accounts section wants sales staff to do more about overdue payments. Clerks in the personnel department cannot understand why clerks in the finance department are paid on a higher scale than they are. Why do managers have their own dining room? And so on. Such conflict hinders the cooperation and coordination that is necessary to the effectiveness of the organisation.

ACTIVITY 11.6   Describe a conflict situation you have encountered between two groups.

Conflict between groups in organisations can be tackled by employing strategies similar to those used to resolve conflict within a group. This would include adopting shared goals and recognising the organisation's goals rather than departmental ones. Developing cooperation and coordination through shared activities and increased communication and interaction between departments will help to alleviate an environment of conflict.

11.3   SUMMARY

Group development:

Tuckman's model:

- Forming
- Storming

- Norming
- Performing

Group behaviour:

- The effect of size and structure
- Norms and conformity
- Groupthink
- Group polarisation
- Conflict in groups and between groups

12 MAKING GROUPS WORK

12.1 EFFECTIVE GROUPS

As discussed in Chapter 9, three factors influence the way a group behaves:

- The group itself.
- Its function or task.
- The context or environment in which it operates.

We shall now examine these in turn to identify how they contribute to the effectiveness of groups.

The Group Itself

Link: teamworking

We have already examined the composition and structure of groups: the appropriateness of size, the need for roles to be fulfilled in order not only to complete the task but also to maintain the group, the importance of a balanced and mixed group. We have also looked at the purpose of norms and conformity in building up group identity and strengthening the cohesiveness of the group, that is, binding the group together to form a closeknit and unified working team.

The interaction and communication between members are essential aspects of an effective group. There must be commitment to the group and its function, and a willingness to participate fully. Mutual trust and support is vital. Members must be willing to listen to each other, to share and value each others' contributions. Everyone must feel able to express their opinion, and to disagree when necessary. The group must foster an open atmosphere and develop the ability to face and resolve conflicts. Groups, as well as individuals, benefit from a degree of social interaction between members to help smooth relationships and promote understanding. Stable membership will enable the group to develop and grow together.

Leadership style is an important factor in how a group behaves and its effectiveness (see Chapter 4). The motivation of the members of the group (Chapter 7) will also affect their degree of commitment and participation.

ACTIVITY 12.1   In Case 12 (Tulip International – Chapter 8) why is there a reluctance to stagger break times on the production lines?

Function or Task

If a group is to function effectively it must have a clear picture of what its function is and its relevance. Objectives must be set and understood by all. Individuals will feel more involved if they take part in setting the goals towards which the group is working. Similarly people find it very difficult to be committed to something of which they cannot see the relevance, but all too often tasks are carried out by individuals and groups who have no idea how those tasks fit into the whole operation or why they are important. It is important that all members of the group are committed to the task and understand their part in achieving the objectives.

If the group is to carry out a task well it must know how to assess its own performance on that task. It must know what the standards are in terms of quality, quantity, time for completion and so on, depending on the nature of the task to be carried out.

Cohesiveness is spoken of a great deal in relation to the effectiveness of groups. It centres particularly on group identity and unity. It will add to the cohesiveness of the group if the group feels that it 'owns' the task and has control over it. Individuals who recognise the value of their own part in carrying out the task will experience greater satisfaction and this will add to the successful integration of the work of all the members. Success or the 'feel good factor' is just as important to groups as to individuals. In groups that believe they are successful, morale will be high and members will experience greater satisfaction. Cohesiveness is enhanced as members feel pleased and proud to be part of the group.

ACTIVITY 12.2   In Case 16 (CarnaudMetalbox – Chapter 9), in which ways did the autonomous teams have control over their work?

Context or Environment

If a group is to be effective it must receive support from outside, that is, from the organisation. It must be recognised as a group and needs to be certain of its place and status within the organisation, and for these to be acknowledged by the organisation. Its achievements and successes should be recognised and where appropriate rewarded.

Factors such as clearly defined goals, roles and structure, mutual trust and cooperation, and good communication are as important in the organisational context and in the relationship between the organisation and the group as they are within the group itself. A management style gives support and encouragement will enhance the effectiveness of the group.

Management has a particular function where relationships between groups are concerned. Allocation of resources, determination of pay scales and so on must be fair and seen to be fair in order to avoid some of the obvious areas of conflict. Management must actively foster and encourage cooperation between departments and sections. This also depends upon the management team being able to resolve its own conflicts and work together in harmony and cooperation.

ACTIVITY 12.3 At CARNAUDMETALBOX (Case 16 – Chapter 9), what were the differences between the management's strategy before the 1980s and the strategies adopted after the 1980s?

12.2 THE IMPORTANCE OF GROUPS

To the Individual

For the individual, the group fulfills a social need. For many workers social interaction is the most important part of groups at work. It is primarily through this that individuals obtain a sense of belonging and identity. Within the group, workers give support, help and advice to each other. The group may offer the individual protection and safety – from other workers, managers or other aspects of the work environment.

Through the group the individual is able to measure his or her performance against that of others and to adopt acceptable levels of output and behaviour. A great deal of work-based learning takes place in the work group, particularly when new workers join the group or when new systems and procedures are introduced.

At times the group may limit or restrict an individual's personal objectives. An individual confined to a particular role within a group may find this frustrating. A worker keen to progress may have no opportunity to display individual qualities and skills and may simply be 'lost' within the group. In some cases individuals feel they have to 'go along' with the group in order to preserve an acceptable working relationship, even though they feel unhappy with the standards set or the attitudes held by the group.

To the Organisation

Sometimes the social interaction within a work group may grow to such an extent that the amount of work done is severely reduced. Workgroup norms on output levels may restrict productivity. A strongly cohesive group may aggravate conflict with other groups. Good workers may be pressured so that neither they nor the organisation benefit from their potential.

In general, however, groups benefit organisations. Effective work groups have lower staff turnover and less absenteeism. Groups can promote better working relationships and communication. Group norms can raise productivity or maintain it at a high level. Groups offer a means of promoting and dispensing learning amongst their members and of maintaining standards through mutual support and encouragement. Many organisations have discovered the value of encouraging groups to appraise and monitor their own performance, as well as solve problems and suggest improvements (as happens in quality circles).

Within a group, innovation and creativity may be increased simply because the members are able to develop and contribute to each others' ideas. This is particularly effective when the members have different types of expertise. Brainstorming is a popular method of generating ideas in groups. In some situations a group can achieve more than the sum of what its members are able to do individually (this is called *synergy*).

Organisations can use groups to build and develop their culture or organisational climate, and through groups organisations may be able to manage change more effectively.

ACTIVITY 12.4   1.   What were the benefits of work groups to the workers at Tulip International (Case 12 – Chapter 8)?

2.   What were the benefits of the autonomous teams to the company at CarnaudMetalbox (Case 16 – Chapter 9)?

12.3   SUMMARY

Effective groups:

● The group itself
● Its function or task
● The context or environment in which it operates

Importance of groups to the individual:

● Social
● Safety, security
● Performance guide
● Learning

Importance of groups to the organisation:

● Lower staff turnover
● Less absenteeism
● Better working relationships
● Communication
● Creativity
● Culture and climate

PORTFOLIO ASSIGNMENT

In order to fulfil the GNVQ Evidence Indicators you should select *either* Method A *or* Method B as your means of carrying out this assignment.

Method A

The objective of this part of the assignment is to carry out a group task, during which you will record in a diary the development and behaviour of the group.

The suggested group size is 5–7 individuals and possible tasks are as follows:

● To raise money for charity.
● To produce a newsheet to be distributed in school or college.
● To set up and run a business activity.

- To put on an exhibition about GNVQ.
- To arrange a visit.

(On a full-time course it may be possible for this activity to be undertaken across several units. In this case the actual task will relate to the other units involved. Units providing possible links are as follows:

- Mandatory: marketing; business planning.
- Optional: creative marketing communications; administrative operations; product development and realisation.
- Additional: sales; teamwork.)

Method B

At your place of work, select a workgroup of which you are a member. Ideally the group should consist of not more than seven members.

Tasks to be Carried Out by Both A and B

Task 1

Keep a diary of the group's activities and behaviour (students following Method A should keep a *group* diary.) The purpose of the diary is to record:

- The progress of the group in carrying out the task.
- The targets and objectives set.
- The relevant stages of the group's development.
- The roles undertaken by the members of the group (task-related and group maintenance roles).
- Observations of the behaviour of the group.
- Conflicts and differences and how they are dealt with.
- The methods and approaches used by the group in order to achieve the targets and objectives set.

Task 2

On completion of the task or at the end of the time allowed, each student should write a report on the behaviour of the group of which she or he is a member. The report should include:

- A description of the type and nature of the group and the context in which it operated.
- A description of the roles undertaken by the members of the group (task-related and group maintenance roles).
- An account of the behaviour of the group (this may include aspects of its development, norms, explanations of what worked well within the group and of where the group experienced difficulties or conflicts and how they were or were not resolved).
- The approaches and methods used by the group in order to fulfil the task (for example setting goals, planning, support and encouragement, sharing and participation).

Points to Note

- The diary is your research document. You must therefore aim to be honest and accurate in what you record.
- Support and encouragement is vital in group work.
- It is important to recognise your own weaknesses and to acknowledge others' strengths and contribution (not just the other way round).
- Conflicts and disagreements are inevitable (and should be recorded) but how you (the group) tackle and resolve them is what matters.

Task 3: Case Study

Wallpaper PLC manufactures wallpapers for the UK retail market. The senior management structure is shown at the top of the organisation chart (Figure 12.1). Each director heads a division of the company. The second part of the chart shows the structure of the sales division. Additional information about the sales division:

- The sales office manager, stock control clerk and order clerks all work in one open plan office (the sales office).
- The stock control clerk works closely with the warehouse staff regarding availability of stock, ordering of stock, deliveries and so on.
- Every Monday morning the sales director, sales office manager and senior sales representative meet briefly to discuss plans for the week and any problems that have arisen.
- Every alternate Wednesday afternoon the sales director attends a directors' meeting.
- Once a month a sales meeting is held. All the sales representatives attend, as does the sales office manager. The sales director chairs

the meeting. The monthly sales figures are reviewed, the next month's targets agreed, and any problems (such as late deliveries, complaints, overdue payments) are discussed.
- The warehouse supervisor is on the health and safety committee.
- The senior sales representative and one of the order clerks are members of the same tennis club.

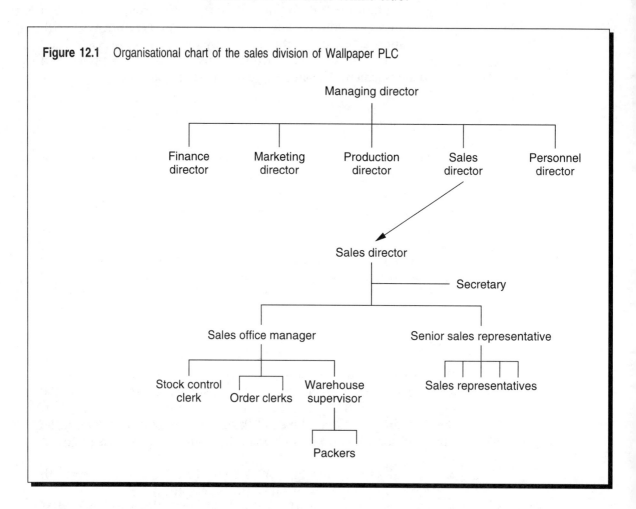

Figure 12.1　Organisational chart of the sales division of Wallpaper PLC

Questions:

1. From the organisation chart and the additional information given, identify and explain the different types of group in the sales division of Wallpaper PLC.
2. In the past customer complaints have been dealt with in a fairly haphazard way. The company now plans to set up a team that will meet regularly to investigate any complaints received and

discuss ways of improving product quality and increasing customer satisfaction. What sort of approach or approaches do you think this group should adopt in order to fulfil its objectives?

3. Three volunteers from the staff of the sales division have agreed to arrange this year's Christmas dinner. How would you expect this group to approach its task? Why would its approach be different from that of the group in question 2?

REFERENCES AND SUGGESTIONS FOR FURTHER READING

Alberdi, L. di, *People, Psychology and Business* (Cambridge: Cambridge University Press, 1990).

Argyle, M., *The Social Psychology of Work* (London: Penguin, 1989).

Cole, G. A., *Management Theory and Practice* (London: DP Publications, 1993).

Evans, D., *Supervisory Management* (London: Cassell, 1986).

Handy, C. B., *Understanding Organizations* (Harmondsworth: Penguin, 1976).

Mullins, L., *Management and Organisational Behaviour* (London: Pitman, 1993).

Peters, T., *Liberation Management* (London: Pan, 1993).

Sallis, E. and Sallis, K., *People in Organisations* (London: Macmillan, 1988).

Index